To Janet
With all my
love
Larissa 1987

Down To Earth

Down To Earth

Canadian Potters at Work

TEXT BY JUDY THOMPSON ROSS

PHOTOGRAPHS BY DAVID ALLEN

RESEARCH BY NINA CZEGLEDY-NAGY

NELSON/CANADA

Published in 1980
by Nelson Canada Limited

Canadian Cataloguing in Publication Data

Main entry under title:
Down to earth

ISBN 0-17-600774-1 bd.
0-17-601463-2 pa.

1. Potters – Canada – Interviews. I. Ross, Judy, 1942- II. Allen, David, 1947-

NK4200.D68 738′.092′2 C80-094751-7

PRINTED AND BOUND IN CANADA

Many people play a part over the years in a project such as this. In the conceptual stage Jeanette Sayers played an instrumental role. Gordon Barnes acted as an advisor in the early days, as did Luke Lindoe, Les Manning, David Cheval, Robin Hopper and Maurice Savoie. We would like to acknowledge and thank the Canada Council for their Explorations grant which enabled us to do the research and travel involved in creating this book. We are indebted to the potters on these pages who gave us much more than their time. They opened their homes, welcomed us at their dining tables, and provided us with many memorable adventures throughout our travels. We are grateful to John and Caroline Finley for their unlimited hospitality during our stay in Nova Scotia. Bill Hushion believed in the book when it was merely an idea, and we thank him for letting us make it a reality. Donald Webster honoured us by writing the historical foreword, and Frank Newfeld's exceptional sense of design speaks for itself on these pages. To our families, our spouses and children, who endured us, survived without us, and encouraged us, we are more than thankful. And finally, we would like to dedicate this book to potters everywhere in Canada with the hope that they will continue to thrive.

JUDY ROSS

Toronto

Contents

Foreword

A few years back I had occasion to serve as a juror for the National Ceramics Exhibition at the Alberta-Glenbow Institute in Calgary. At the time I was reluctant, for I had not potted in years and was a hesitant amateur. Neither had I ever been exposed to such a vast array of contemporary studio ceramics all in one room, much less been called upon to render judgements.

The exhibit pointed up to me how dramatically ceramic technology and engineering have advanced over the past century, in materials, techniques and equipment. The range of possibilities open to the contemporary potter was unimaginable even beyond fantasy to the commercial craft potter of the 19th century, and this was clearly evident in even a cursory perusal of the entries for that exhibition.

To one who has excavated and studied the works and technology of earlier Canadian operations such as the Brantford (Ontario) Stoneware Pottery (1849-1907), the Oswald Hornsby Pottery (Charlottetown, PEI, 1879-1898) or the William Eby Pottery (Conestoga, Ontario, 1855-1906), the impact of this advance is staggering. Even the late 19th-century potters worked in ways little changed in centuries. They used natural red-earthen and stoneware clays, for they had nothing else. They dug it, screened and cleaned it and prepared it for the wheel themselves. They had no idea of the components of their clays, and thus no idea of proper firing temperatures. They had no pyrometric cones and thus no way of judging firing temperatures anyway, other than experience and heat colour – dull red, glowing red, orange, yellow, or white. Without gas or electricity, or even oil or coal, they fired with wood in outdoor kilns, a process that sometimes took days. Little wonder that waste often approached 50% of production, and sometimes more.

These potters, likewise, had nothing approaching the range of modern glazes and enamels. For linings and coatings they were limited to natural slips. Glazes were based on lead oxide, soluble and toxic, and a few metallic oxide colorants – iron, copper, tin and manganese.

Still, in spite of their technical limitations, these potters made some extremely pleasant and fine pieces. I could say the same of much 18th-century English earthenware, and even some basically utilitarian Medieval pottery. Antiquity or modernity has nothing to do with quality of expression. I can think of some five hundred and even thousand-year-old pots that would likely have gained three or four juror votes at the Calgary exhibition.

Though contemporary ceramic materials and methodology have emerged through a technological revolution after centuries of little change, good proportion and form and plain good taste have not. Potters, like other artist-craftsmen, follow underlying sensibilities, one being tradition versus imagination, the two often being incompatible. An appreciation of form and good taste can conflict as well, and often does, with a sense of flair and style. The results, in ceramics, can be anything from absolute brilliance to pure kitsch.

If age and technology have little bearing on the merit of ceramics as a decorative art form, what does? It all still comes down, perhaps, to the basic judgement and co-

Foreword

gency of the individual potter; some have it, some do not. Technical skill, of course, can be developed with experience. Whether the other sensibilities can I am not sure.

The commercial craft potter of the 19th century and earlier typically produced one form until his planned inventory, perhaps several hundred virtually identical pieces, was complete. Then he would switch to another form. He also accumulated a full kiln load of greenware, perhaps a month's work at the wheel, before he fired. Artisan rather than artist (the distinction mostly a matter of intent), he was a full-time and thoroughly competent and professional potter, day in and day out. With complete rapport with his material, the early commercial potter produced routinely and repetitively, and followed tradition and habit-pattern far more than his own imagination. As a result, however, his products often had an understated beauty and excellence born of gradual evolution of forms.

The contemporary studio potter, conversely, often acts as an artist, lavishing great imagination, utmost skill and considerable time on a single piece. Certainly he experiments far more, and produces over a greater range, than the early craft potter would ever have considered. When the commercial craft potter did experiment or make a special piece, the result was usually at least well within the realm of his own experience. The present-day studio or 'art' potter often goes much further.

Two things seem very evident in the work of many contemporary studio ceramists. One is the still pervasive influence of tradition, English, European or Oriental. Individual imagination may be superimposed on tradition, often very successfully. Escaping tradition altogether, however, seems like escaping gravity; it puts one into strange and sometimes dangerous realms. It almost seems that good taste and form require evolution and development, which would imply, if not mandate, attention to tradition.

Particularly from an antiquarian position, then, I also find myself constantly expanding my own horizons as to what can now be produced with ceramic materials and methods. The early commercial potters, to be sure, often made truly artistic pieces, though the judgement comes only through hindsight. Still, they produced primarily utilitarian wares, for a wholly different market and audience and in a very different domestic economy from that of contemporary potters.

No early potter could have attempted some of the elaborate constructions successfully formed and fired today, or anything that could not be wheel-turned or slip-cast. Certainly mixtures of materials, ceramicized cloth, for example, or extreme ranges of glaze colours and tones, or eggshell-thin porcelains, or component pieces which fit, after firing, almost as if machined, would not have been even remotely possible. By comparison, a great deal of modern studio ceramics are possible now largely because of technological advances. Potters' skills, of course, have expanded and broadened to fully exploit and utilize the materials and technology available.

Whether the whole state of the art has really advanced as much as the best of contemporary ceramics would lead us to believe is difficult to assess. Discounting industry, working with clay is still working with clay, as it has always been. Regardless of the materials and equipment, potting is still a very basic and personal thing. Perhaps, then, the contemporary ceramist really has much more in common with the potter of five hundred or a thousand years ago than we realize, or is immediately evident from comparing products.

But comparing products is the only way we can judge. There are no records of the dreams and thoughts of our early commercial potters. Our only perspective of them is through the works that survived or those pieced together from fragments uncovered at excavation sites. At least the historians of the future won't suffer the same lack. As one who has long been involved with the history of pottery in this country, I feel that this book fills an obvious gap in the documentation of the craft, providing a visual and verbal record of the work of Canada's potters today that will become a valuable resource tomorrow.

DONALD BLAKE WEBSTER

Curator, Canadiana Department
Royal Ontario Museum

Introduction

Throughout the history of ceramics in Canada, the focus has been more on the achievement of certain individuals than on the dynamics of a group movement.

In the early part of this century the only potters to achieve international acclaim lived in the Maritimes. Alice Mary Hagen in Nova Scotia, Kjeld and Erica Deichmann of New Brunswick and the Lorenzens of Nova Scotia were all celebrated for their work in clay, but flourished only as individuals without spawning schools or movements for the generations that followed.

But in 1936 a national force in ceramics was born with the founding of the Canadian Guild of Potters in Toronto, Ontario. This group became instrumental in creating an awareness of ceramics across the country, and for forty years furthered our reputation with international exhibitions and awards. That same year, in Quebec, a pottery department was founded at the Ceramic School of Montreal by Pierre Normandeau who trained at Sèvres, France. This department became a training ground for the early pioneers of pottery in that province.

In the western provinces, too, there are long roots in the craft of pottery. It was in 1947 that a ceramics department was started by Luke Lindoe at the Alberta College of Arts in Calgary. Many of our early influences came from this area, with people like Walter Drohan, Ed Drahanchuk and Walter Dexter leading the way. Two years later, the British Columbia Potters Guild was formed, and it is still a moving force in that province.

Many of the organizations and schools founded in the thirties and forties were revitalized by the emergence of the 'back to earth' movements that surfaced and permeated our lives in the mid-sixties. Potters suddenly became acceptable, if not admired, and governments reacted by allotting great sums of money for the development of elaborate ceramics departments in community colleges and universities. This, in turn, attracted potters from other countries, particularly England and the United States, who came here to staff the newly-formed departments. The pottery boom was underway, and with it a whole new generation of craftsmen grew up and went to work. Some have continued to evolve, to influence others, and to create names for themselves in the scattered mosaic of Canadian pottery.

Some of these men and women appear in this book. They have been chosen to represent the variety of work being done, and to illustrate the life of a studio potter in this country. The backgrounds of this group of potters are as varied as the environments they have chosen to inhabit. It is in these environments that they are depicted here, beginning in the pottery studios of the west coast and moving east to the potters of Nova Scotia. They are seen in their studios, at home and as part of the landscape that surrounds them and influences their work.

Some of them are young and began their careers with the comfort of an establishment to guide them; others were pioneers who persevered in times when pottery was an unknown art in our society. All of them survive without a supportive tradition in our culture and, in most cases, without the accolades awarded to other artists such as painters and sculptors. Despite these

Introduction

restrictions they continue to work with clay, struggling to master the craft which has been called 'the most difficult of all the arts'.

Ceramics is a unique blend of art and science and is one of the oldest crafts in history. The plastic quality of clay lends itself to a multitude of artistic interpretations and its responsive nature readily reflects the imprint of the maker so that every piece becomes a personal statement. The required technical knowledge far exceeds that of any other art form, and the inexhaustible possibilities span centuries and the civilizations of the past. In many countries ceramics has always been considered an art form equal in value to painting and sculpture, but in the modern Western world we are just beginning to recognize pottery as a valid contribution to our culture.

In Canada we have potters of international stature who have won acclaim for their work in different countries. Many of them are on these pages; some are not, for reasons dictated solely by the confines of a book not large enough to encompass them all. The potters chosen here represent the diversity of the craft, from the functional domestic ware of Roger Kerslake to the unique conceptual forms of Annemarie Schmid Esler; from the sensitive sculptural pieces of Maurice Savoie to the industrial dinnerware designed and created by Gaétan Beaudin.

The purpose of this book is to further the knowledge and appreciation of ceramics as an art form by giving voice to these artists who work with clay. They can best describe their own motives, their philosophies and their concepts of clay. They live in different areas of Canada, but their work does not offer any obvious regional distinctions. The environment, although influential, seems less of a factor than the innate artistic inspiration of the individual. These are all people who can see in a lump of formless clay the possibility of a finished pot. A sensitive spirit and a dedication to beauty distinguish them as individuals, and these are embodied in the fine quality of their work. It is hoped that their words as well as their work will be a source of inspiration to art lovers everywhere.

Wayne Ngan

Wayne Ngan

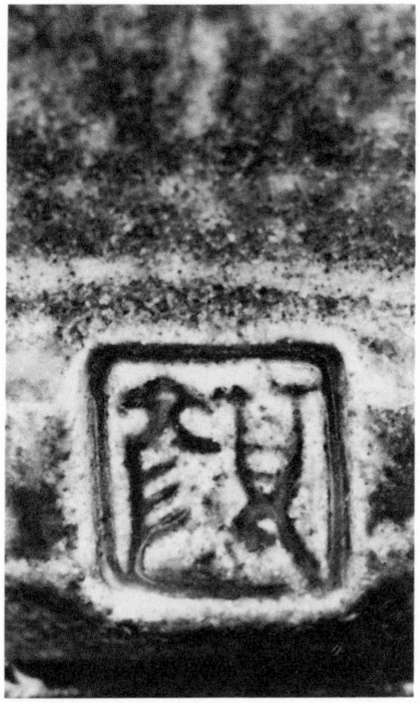

Life for Wayne Ngan is a continuing quest for simplicity, for a return to the most basic and primitive in all things. His pottery, his life and the ebb and flow of nature are all inter-woven in the serenity of his Hornby Island home. He lives with his French wife and two young daughters in a small community on this remote Gulf Island which is separated from the mainland of British Columbia by the Straits of Georgia. The natural beauty of Hornby Island, with the sea and rock cliffs, arbutus groves and plentiful wildlife, is a perfect setting for the self-sufficient organic lifestyle of Wayne and his family.

Their home began as two chicken coops pushed together for temporary shelter. Over the years, as needs arose, Wayne built on, using driftwood from the beach and other natural or recycled materials to create a unique sod-roofed home that is as much a part of the landscape as the grassy meadow that surrounds it. A few yards away is Wayne's spacious studio created with the natural curves of the driftwood timbers supporting it. The adjoining kiln shed is a marvel of recycling ingenuity; its fireproof roof is made entirely from salvaged car tops. A garden at the back of the house provides much of the family's food, while there are also oysters, fish and seaweed to be gathered from the ocean.

Wayne believes in giving life and purity to his pottery by using natural elements and avoiding refined or commercial materials. He gathers stones from the beach and grinds them to make glazes. He fires in a big salt kiln that burns wood and oil, often adding seaweed or other natural material to the firing. His goal now is to build a large wood-firing kiln which will further his quest to share more directly in the firing of his work and, therefore, in the life of his pots.

Wayne claims that he'd like to go back 1000 years in time, but he isn't there yet. He is, however, not far from his roots in Canton, China where he was born in 1937. When he was a child, his mother worked all day in the rice paddies, leaving Wayne to survive on his own. When he was hungry, he caught fish by hand in the nearby stream. When he was bored, he dug up clay from the rice fields and made his own toys. He came to Canada in 1951 with his grandfather and studied at the Vancouver College of Art. When he moved to the primitive confines of Hornby Island in 1967, he adapted easily. The art of living to the tune of nature had already been part of his life.

Wayne Ngan

"Working with clay is, I think, part of my nature. It is easy, the most flexible medium I can imagine. Through clay I can touch all four basic elements: earth, water, fire and air, and bring those four elements back to life. When I look out at all the nature around me, it becomes my pottery. I save all my ashes for glazes after cooking. It is a way of life. Everything becomes a part of my elements for pottery. In a sense it is very pleasing; all things become part of you.

I don't like modern technology as it is applied to the Western potter's world, like electric kilns and refined materials. It is so cold. It is like dealing with cardboard, not clay. People make pots that look like cardboard. I really like to start from raw materials and work to a finished pot. What is really important for me is to do some honest work, work which is related to the depth of my understanding.

I would like to dig my own clay, but there is none on this island. I have been hunting for stoneware clay up in northern British Columbia. I found some clay, but it was on private property. It is very hard for a potter. Those people don't understand you; they think maybe you are looking for gold. I told them I am not interested in gold, I am looking for clay! It is a very frustrating experience.

So now I buy clay and sand and mix my own clay body. I can't use clay as it comes in a package. I have to put a little human element back into it by working at it with my feet. It's the same with everything today. Flour, for example. They slowly kill all life in flour and then try to make bread out of it. And the bread tells us exactly what happened; it has no life.

I make all my own tools and put a lot of thought into every one of them. It is a slow approach. It takes a long time to learn how to use a tool and to feel comfortable with it.

Right now I am really interested in white porcelain clay, in making pure shapes with colour and decoration like the Chinese Sung Dynasty and the Yi Dynasty of Korea. My goal is to try to have that kind of quality. I know it is very difficult, partly because of the confusion of our times, partly because of the different materials. It doesn't seem to work that well, but I try anyway.

I am looking for life, for life-giving substances. Like ashes are very good materials for glazes. But the glaze on a pot is only a coat; the beauty that's behind is the clay body, like a soul in a person. Sometimes the person who makes the pot is also a contributing factor. And the fire too. If you have an electric kiln it only radiates heat; it is not live fire. It

Wayne Ngan

doesn't matter how hard you try, what comes out has really a cold-looking surface. It is artificial.

The kiln is like a womb, like a mother. It is a very important part of the elements. I have a gas kiln and an oil and wood kiln. The more I get into pottery the more I like primitive fuels. To me, using an electric kiln is not life; it is just existing. Like the egg and the eggshell; the egg is living and the eggshell is existing. From the outside they look the same, but inside the real thing is not the same. The one is a life force and the other is just existing.

I wanted to build a wood-firing kiln here, so I went to Japan to learn how they do it. But I found they were so secretive. They would never show me a kiln being opened. They would give you their wives before they'd show you the kiln. I don't know why. Maybe they just think you can't get things for nothing.

When I was first in Japan I found everything very interesting – the way they work and so on – but as I got deeper into the whole thing it became different. Those master potters don't think in terms of pots anymore, they think in terms of millions and millions of dollars behind the production. In the beginning they were interested in pottery, but the commercial thing is so powerful it drives them to the materialistic side. The humble potter becomes buried slowly.

One day I arrived at this master potter's place in Japan and I said I would like to see him. They told me he was working so I waited in this damn cold and after a long while I asked, "Where is the master potter?" They said, "Oh, he is watching TV." Here I was hanging around, my hands almost frozen, and he is watching TV! The apprentices are so protective; like the master is God. While they're firing *his* kiln he's watching TV. It becomes an unhealthy life.

So I never did find out about wood-firing kilns in Japan. I will have to invent one myself. I want a big three or four chamber one, but I have to be able to stoke it myself and only from one side. So it will have to fit my sleeping schedule.

I am always seeking something I cannot do in the pottery field. I taught myself salt glazing. It is slow, but right now anything is possible for me in salt glazing. When the temperature gets up to about cone 7 I start to throw bits of wood into the kiln. Then when the salt is thrown in, the sodium and silica combine and slowly become sticky. Then I introduce some dry seaweed or ashes. It is invisible – you can't see what is happening inside. If someone gives me some special wood which I don't have or hazelnuts, I throw them in. Sometimes I throw in orange peels, apples, old sweaters. It's all OK. It's a way to deal with the life inside there. There are no rules when you don't train in the traditional way. Everything is possible. You cut your hair and throw it in. A lot of people call it recycling. I just use everything. My things go back to my pottery.

The problem with my life is not enough time. I work longer hours than most people and I get no help. My wife has different interests. We have a lot in common, but professionally we lead two different lives. She is a weaver and a painter and she's not interested in pottery. When I go back to the house from the studio I would like a little rest, but I get involved in carrying wood, doing household chores, cooking food. It is not the same as in Japan where the master potter doesn't have to do anything but make pots. Japan is a man's world. My wife would never stand for it. Here my wife is more the man than me. Even the children are busy creating things. The problem with this family is everyone is too creative. Nobody wants to do the chores.

There is always a lot to do with this house. There are constant changes. To me a life is not a complete statement. I find my life is in a constant moving process of being. Every day I have ten different projects in my head and I really don't know which way to go. It is very interesting, but I feel I have already lived six lives. And I still need more.

The way we live here makes me feel, in a sense, like I am still a child. When I was young, I collected copper pieces and glass and similar things to sell so I could buy candy. Here I do the same. I go through the garbage dump and look for building parts and I go to the beach and look for certain kinds of wood for building. It is a kind of scrounging and yet it is part of my nature. On the other hand, some of these things you could not buy even if you had the money. The driftwood which has come from a live tree, has been washed by rain and storm in the sea, has then drifted back and forth and been blasted by the sand, has a kind of life which no human hand can give to it. For me it is unique.

I love all parts of being a potter, except the business side. I am not a businessman. I have some places like the Vancouver Art Gallery which sell my work, but I really don't make much money. I guess I really need an agent. At least I can part with my work now. I don't mind selling things. When I first started doing pottery I was so intimate with my work I couldn't sell anything. I used to sleep with my pots."

Wayne Ngan

Robin Hopper

Robin Hopper

Robin Hopper is a contented man. He is alive with enthusiasm for his life, his work and his Eden-like surroundings in Metchosin, British Columbia where he has lived in a rebuilt farmhouse with his wife, Sue, and their three children since moving from Ontario in 1977. Minutes from the Pacific shores on Vancouver Island, the Hoppers' home is set amongst towering Douglas fir trees that typify the splendour of this region. Their home was planned to suit the casual 'open house' lifestyle that has been a Hopper trademark for years. Their easy-going hospitality attracts people from across the country. On any night there may be a dozen or so people gathered around the long pine table in the dining room. And on those days when the pottery shop adjacent to the house is open, students and shoppers file through and marvel at the success of this operation. The Hoppers sell enough pottery from their tiny showroom to support themselves without the need of additional sales outlets.

Their success, however, has not come from a casual approach, but from gruelling hard work. Robin approaches his craft in a calculated and methodical way. Armed with a vast knowledge of ancient ceramic techniques and an inquisitive mind that absorbs the rhythms of his environment, he combines these with his own abundant energy to maintain an impressively high level of production. Sixteen-hour days are not uncommon. But every morning starts with a walk to the nearby Witty Lagoon through musky wooded paths leading down to the sea. This is a contemplative time for Robin and Sue, a necessary break from the active pace of maintaining the pottery. It is a time to enjoy the beauty of the landscape and the shifting moods of forest, lake and seashore.

In 1977 Robin became the first recipient of the Saidye Bronfman Award for Excellence in the Crafts. The award required him to produce a major exhibit of his work to travel across the country. Robin's exhibit was a tribute to his love of Canada. Titled 'Explorations within a Landscape', it included 67 pieces evoking the landscapes of the western provinces and reflecting Robin's exploration of the ancient Chinese pottery methods of agateware and neriage.

Born in Surrey, England in 1939, Robin studied printmaking and ceramics at college and then worked in theatre design before starting his own pottery studio in Berkshire. He immigrated to Canada in 1968. His first years here were spent teaching at Central Technical School in Toronto and Georgian College in Barrie, and maintaining a full-time pottery production at the same time. This would have been an almost impossible workload without the help of Sue, who has been the backbone of the operation throughout their married life. For years she has done the bookkeeping, the organizing, the 'joe jobs'. But now that the children are older, she has started making her own pots as well as helping Robin in the production of their 'bread and butter' functional wares. With her help, Robin has the time and freedom to explore new directions and develop his own one-of-a-kind pieces.

Robin Hopper

"I love to work with clay. Each time I sit down with a piece of clay it becomes another challenge. Being a potter is a very exciting profession. You also get the secondary benefit of people enjoying what you have made and this is a tremendous source of energy return. I think any young person coming out of college can make it as a full-time potter if they don't mind working reasonably hard.

This was part of my aim in setting up the ceramics program at Georgian College. I wanted to train students to become self-supporting potters, technicians or teachers. In 1973 I gave up teaching myself partly because it became obvious that I couldn't carry on with so many hours of work without cracking up somewhere down the line, but also because there was hardly anybody out in the field making a decent income from being a full-time craftsman. I thought it must be possible, so that's what I did. For a long time I had four full-time assistants. Sue looked after the showroom, did packing and shipping and kept the books. And I just worked like crazy.

A lot depends on your income expectations. I don't make a fortune, but I do have a very good income, and I'm happy with what I am doing. It is incredible to me that you can live where you want to live, do what you want to do and still make a decent income doing it. Can you have it any better than that?

We don't have any apprentices now. I have been through the stage of mass production in terms of having a large production studio. When we moved out here to Vancouver Island I wanted to slow down a little. I wasn't comfortable with large-scale production any more. Now I want to be able to explore a lot more, to work in different directions.

I like to work in series. The landscape series actually started back in Ontario. The earliest were snow landscapes. I used to drive back and forth to Barrie and I guess there was an unconscious blending with my visual imagination. Having been a printmaker, I've always been interested in combining the two aspects of printmaking and clay. I became conscious of wanting to work with flattened forms, big slabs or big plates, and then use the surface as a canvas.

The design techniques that I used on the landscape series were partly a result of all the glaze testing I did at Georgian College. When I went to art school technology was taboo. You graduated thinking that clay came in plastic bags and glazes appeared from the basement in different buckets. I found out how little I knew when I set up my own studio. I decided then that if I ever got into a teaching situation I was going to stress technical aspects like mad.

Robin Hopper

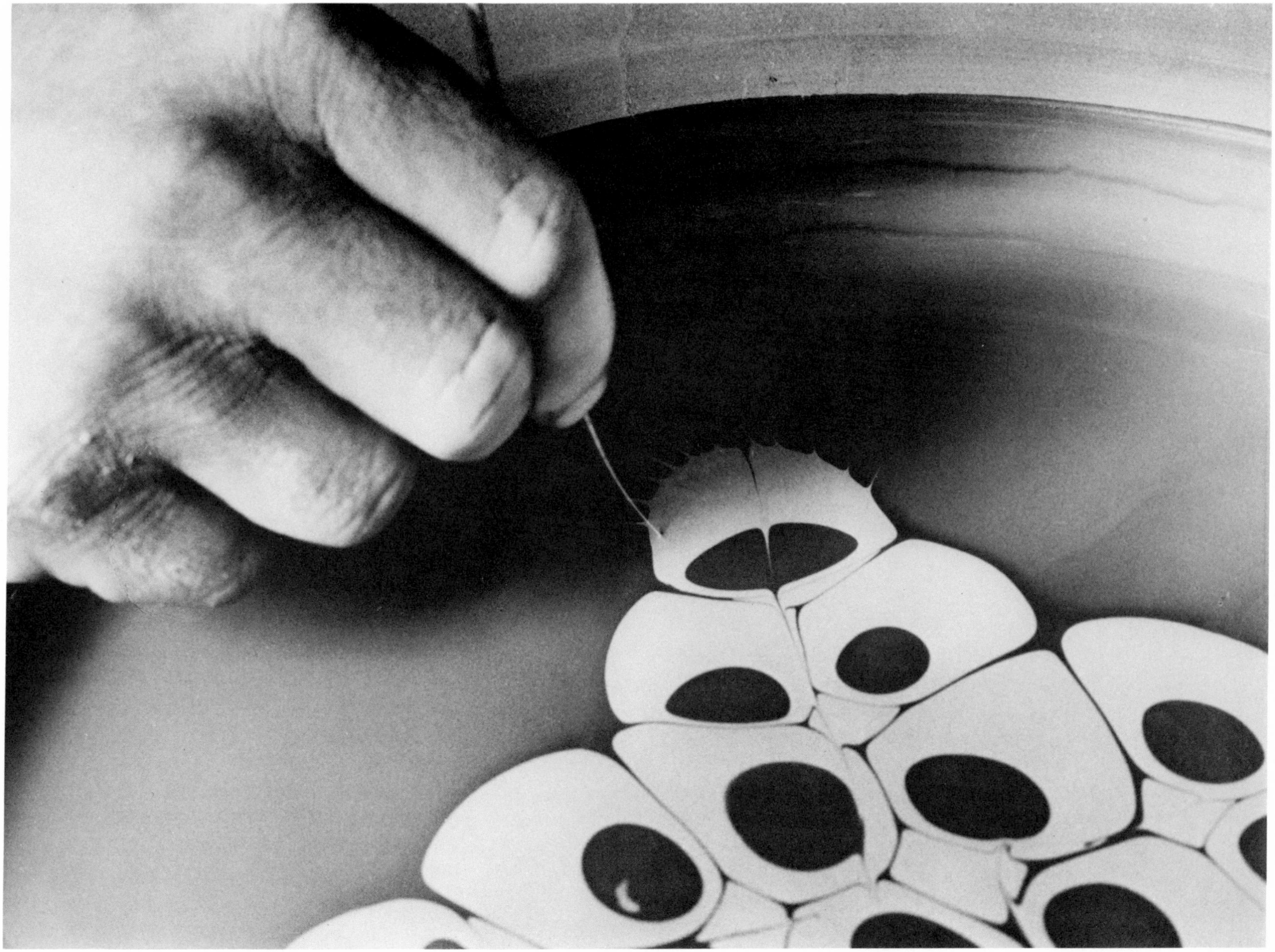

Robin Hopper

Robin Hopper

Robin Hopper

When I was at Georgian I got to see about 30,000 different glaze tests that my students were working on. I have a fairly retentive memory, so when I got home I wrote down the things I found interesting. So I had all this glaze information in my head and on paper and when we moved across Canada I took visual notes of the colours of the landscape. I carried a little notebook and wrote down what I saw. We drove through the prairies in the rain and the fields were sort of washed-out goldy yellow colours and the sky went from bluish grey to pink. There were some really beautiful colour combinations and I could make a quick analysis of the colours and write down an appropriate glaze recipe.

When I got out here to Victoria the colours were incredible. Because of the proximity of water you get a lot of vapours in the atmosphere that change the direction of the sun's rays. This has an amazing effect on colour, producing soft pinky greys, turquoisey pastels. Then when I started to work on the Bronfman show I decided to explore this Canadian landscape and use all of this accumulated information. I feel very Canadian, even though I was born in England. My work is totally Canadian.

I probably have 50 glazes I use on a regular basis and almost every kiln load that goes through has a new series of glaze tests in it, so there is always a change. I tend to work in series, much like a printmaker. I make a whole lot of pots of all different shapes and bisque them until I have enough of a balance of what I would like for an exhibition. Then I take a group of maybe a half-dozen big plates, a half-dozen small plates, some tall vases, altogether maybe 40 or 50 in one group. I apply one glaze at a time on every piece. On some I may put up to eight different glazes. They are like overlays in printing, so you gradually build up a vision. Then the whole series is fired at one time and I may never do that series again.

I use every different method of glaze application that I know of, except spray. I trail, sponge, pour, stipple, brush, dip. And I've done a lot of work on slip decoration. When I taught a Ceramic History course I discovered a lot of techniques that were somehow lost or forgotten in the past and I use a lot of those.

I have a split personality as far as pottery is concerned. I do a lot of functional ware in a very traditional style, but I also do a lot of one-of-a-kind things. The functional ware gives us bread and butter and the others put the cream on the top. For me, it's a nice balance. I usually have two or three one-man shows a year and try to balance it out so they're about four months apart. For about two months prior to an exhibition I just concentrate

on the pieces for that show and usually make about four or five times more pots than I need. I don't necessarily select the best pots, because I'm more concerned with the overall effect. I am familiar with most of the spaces where I show, so I just visualize the space and work accordingly. For the Bronfman show I made about 500 pieces and selected 67.

Sue has been incredibly supportive and helpful. Frankly, without her, I don't know what I would have done. We do a range of functional ware between us that sells so well it must be satisfying the needs of the market. I am very analytical about functional ware. If a teapot is to be made, it has to function as such. The mugs I make today took 10 years to develop. When I was in art school they talked about the 'golden mean', the system of proportions that relate to the human form. It has been found that work based on the golden mean is pleasing to 95% of the population. I think this is an interesting concept, because if one uses it in design you will please more people. I started to use it back in college days and now it's intuitive. For instance, the basic breakdown of a mug should have the top section a third of the total and the handle should span two thirds. The curve of the lip fits my bottom lip and the decoration covers a third of the surface. The size of the handle is important. I used to ask people at workshops if they held a mug with one finger, two fingers or three fingers, or with their whole fist. There are several variations. You can't satisfy them all, but if you're somewhere in the middle you're OK. A lot of the work that I've done has been thought out that analytically. It means that most people are very comfortable with my work, even if they don't know why.

Apart from pottery, gardening interests me most. Living out here is like coming to paradise for a gardener. We've spent a lot of time planning the garden here so that we have different things in bloom all year round. There's something very special about developing a garden. It is an ongoing process.

I guess if I couldn't do pottery I'd want to be a landscape gardener or something, but I can't imagine ever getting tired of pottery. Bernard Leach once said, "If you change your mind every second day for a period of not less than 80 years, you need never cover the same ground twice. Such is the breadth of materials with which we deal in ceramics." There is such an infinite variety of earth materials, of temperatures, of interactions taking place in oxidation and reduction. It is incredible. It is the most complex of art forms and I can't see how anybody could every be bored with it. I find it an endlessly exciting craft."

Byron Johnstad

Byron Johnstad

At the age of twenty-one, Byron Johnstad was working in New York as a product designer and was growing steadily more unhappy at the drawing board. Instead of designing things that somebody was going to make, he wanted to be involved in the making process himself. Not knowing exactly what he wanted to do, he took a selection of craft books out of the library. The book on ceramics impressed him and he decided to become a potter. Although he could not remember ever handling a lump of clay, he thought that this medium presented the greatest manual challenge. The next day he quit his job, returned to his hometown of Chicago and enroled in the ceramics program at the Art Institute.

Byron has made dramatic and instinctive decisions like this many times during his adult life. A few years ago he put aside everything, including pottery, to take a year off. It took him five days to make the decision. He enroled in a personal discovery program at the Cold Mountain Institute on Cortes Island, British Columbia, not knowing whether he would ever work with clay again.

But recently, Byron has been reshaping his life and renewing his interests as a potter. He now lives in Lantzville, a tiny community on Vancouver Island not far from Nanaimo. His home, where he works in an airy basement with many windows, is just a few minutes walk from a rocky beach looking out on the Straits of Georgia. For eight years he was a full-time studio potter. but now finds teaching part-time at Nanaimo's Malaspina College a welcome diversion from the solitude of working and living alone.

His work, functional stoneware reduction fired in a gas kiln, is most outstanding for its brushed-on oxide decoration. The sureness of his brushwork creates strong vibrant pieces that reflect in form and feeling his Scandinavian heritage. In the early days Byron's pots were simple, functional and undecorated. He discovered brushwork by accident and has been decorating with oxides of cobalt, iron and rutile ever since.

Byron Johnstad

"I was using a white glaze for a couple of years and suddenly I had problems with it. So I decided to test a new white glaze. I was going to make a simple test on a little bowl and it occured to me that maybe oxides would do something interesting to the glaze. So I mixed up some cobalt and some iron and a bit of rutile and did a couple of brush-strokes and stuck it into the kiln. When it came out the colour was so vivid that I suddenly realized I'd been ignoring decoration for too long. The first pieces were very clumsy, but it evolved, and from then on I never stopped. I just kept doing it.

Sometimes now I get bored with brush decoration. But the problem is I became it and it has become part of me. I tried when I first came back from a year off to do something different, but some of the shops I'd been dealing with would not even buy my new things. I had such a good reputation with my decorated work that it was hard to say to hell with it and do something else and starve. There are subtle changes taking place in my pots now that reflect the changes in me since my year away. I am softer now – not as rigid as I used to be – and my forms are softening. My decoration for a time was extremely tight and controlled. I would do some brushwork and then outline that pattern with another line. Everything stayed where it was supposed to be. My life needed that at the time. I wanted to control everything because everything was drifting apart. Now I can look at my pots and say, "OK, I want to break away from those edges, I don't want to be outlined any more. I want to move across the forms. I want to be open and looser."

I've never had a love affair with clay. I enjoy many materials and fibres. I have done a lot of weaving. I have worked in wood as a furniture designer, and lately I've been working with paper pulp. Clay is just the thing I place the dominant emphasis on and have explored to the greatest degree. But there are times when I cannot go into my studio for a week. Finally I get myself down there and once I get started it just goes.

I studied product design before I ever got into clay and that is still a part of me. I was very much out of the Bauhaus school and for a long time the idea that form follows function stayed with me. So even now when I'm exploring extruded forms and more sculptural shapes, they still tend to be functional in that they have an opening and can be used. They can still be containers.

Part of the challenge to me is to design a form that also works. I enjoy cooking and when I make something which should function in the cooking process I have some sense of what it should look like and how it should work. I'm always trying to come up

with new ideas for functional pots. For the last year I've been working on large serving plates – wide platters with a wide rim and a lid. I fire them separately so I don't have to have an unglazed edge on the platter rim. Then, when it is used for serving, it doesn't look as if it's missing a lid. Some cooking vessels really don't function, like casseroles with very rigid corners and inward turning flanges that are just horrors to clean. They must be made by potters who never had to clean potatoes au gratin out of a casserole. The only way I can keep making the same functional ware is to be constantly exploring the forms, finding new ways to do the same thing.

I am somewhat cyclical in the way I work. In the past I was working in such small spaces that I had to throw at one time, and then bisque, and then glaze and so on. Now I have the space to break out of that, but I am comfortable in the routine. When I have a glaze firing going I do nothing but watch the kiln. It's not because of the kiln; it practically fires itself. It is just that my concentration is centred on it. When a kiln load is finished I usually relax for a few days, and get right away from it.

I thrive on change and on visual stimulation. I am a media freak. I constantly look through books, go off to see things, take walks, discover shells. I tend to gather experience in and reach a saturation point. Then it comes out in new forms. I work this way too. I tend to work very hard for a period of time and then do nothing but rest and take things in. All of a sudden I'll hit on something and it starts all over again.

I don't do much direct selling any more. I used to have a little retail shop in front of my house when I lived up in Courtney, B.C. and I sold directly from there. It was right on the Island highway and it became a very profitable situation. I may do the same thing here some day. But right now I sell mainly through shops and occasional commissions. I like dealing directly with customers when I make a dinner set because I can assess their needs that way. Also, by cutting out the middleman I can sell a dinner set for about the same price as a commercial set of dinnerware.

I think success in this business is controlled by a very fickle finger of fate, and in large part it also has to do with one's attitude. I know of potters who produce very fine products, but have very negative personalities. I think their negativism is conveyed in their work and people pick it up and do not buy.

Byron Johnstad

Byron Johnstad

Byron Johnstad

For someone to start in with a pottery of their own today requires a big investment. The price of everything is going up. Take cobalt, for instance. I bought some a couple of months ago and last week it was twice the price. I heard that in the States it was selling for even more and was rationed. It is coming from Africa and that area is in terrible turmoil right now. In a couple of years you may not see much of cobalt blue.

It takes a lot of work to be successful. I have reached a point where I know I am producing a good product and I'm not ashamed of saying it. I don't want to hide under a bushel, and be just a humble potter.

I have traditionally been low priced so people can afford to buy my work. What is it good for if people can't buy it? You end up with a house filled with pots. I make them for people to use and I really dislike it when some customer remarks that something will look good on such and such a shelf. "Oh no, you are going to kill it," I say to myself.

I have worked with assistants over the years but it has never been very successful. One of them didn't like making glazes or loading the kiln or doing any of the menial tasks. He just wanted to make pots and I suddenly realized that I had become *his* assistant. Somewhere the roles had switched. So now I work alone. I can't work effectively with people around me in the studio.

One of the things I find fascinating about being a potter is that my work actually becomes a visual record of where and what I was at the time. I can look at the pots I've produced over the last ten years and see something about myself. I wasn't aware of it at the time, but now I can see, for instance, when my marriage was coming to an end and I was trying to control everything. My pots were all tightly thrown and the drawing was totally contained. Now things are moving, the peripheries are hardly defined anymore. I am breaking out of that rigid aspect, both in my work and in myself. I have become much more spontaneous. Being a typical Virgo who plans everything ad nauseam, I've had to work at getting away from that overly controlled aspect of my personality.

My life does not centre around my wheel. I am a person who is made up of a lot of different facets. I have many interests – cooking, gardening, collecting old Chinese teapots, fixing up my house. I don't want clay to be my whole life. I don't think it's necessary to be obsessed with it to be good at it."

The Landscape of the Potter

Walter Ostrom

Ruth Gowdy McKinley

Roger Kerslake

Robin Hopper

Annemarie Schmid Esler

Annemarie Schmid Esler

Annemarie Schmid Esler plays a trick with our eyes. Her sculptural clay forms deceive us. She takes advantage of the chameleon quality of clay and uses it in non-traditional, often surrealistic ways. Her recent series of 'crows in crates' requires close examination to discover that the crates are made from textured clay, not wood, and that the wounded crows are bandaged not with surgical tape, but with paper-thin slabs of clay.

Several years ago, she became known for her bed and pillow sculptures. Soft and squashy-looking, these pieces defied their true nature of hard, brittle porcelain clay. On other sculptural forms she combines real pieces of rural debris with life-like clay imitations, again challenging our perceptions of what is real.

Her work has progressed through very definable stages. Most of her pieces are closely tied to the western landscape which stretches out in all directions from her hilltop home near Calgary, Alberta. From every window, a different scene unfolds – the burgeoning skyline of Calgary, the largeness of the prairie sky, the rolling foothills of the Rocky Mountains. She lives with her husband Ken (John) Esler, a well-known printmaker, their two sons, an aged St. Bernard dog and three cats.

Both Annemarie and Ken have studios at home. Annemarie works alone in a converted garage where she strives to find enough uninterrupted time to work out her ideas. When she is producing, her energy level peaks, she needs little sleep, and there is nothing else in the world she would rather be doing. A confessed compulsive worker, she maintains that it is best for her and everybody around that all her energies go straight into her work.

Born in Winnipeg in 1937 to German immigrant parents, Annemarie grew up in King's Park, a Winnipeg suburb. The community in those days was a kaleidoscope of people ranging from a sociologist to a grand-motherly Belgian bootlegger, a Russian who was growing black gladiolas, and a colony of Dutch market gardeners. Her mother insisted that Annemarie receive a formal education, but the major influence in her life came for her more free spirited father. He was a 1930's hippie and inventor who grew mushrooms, bred rabbits and fed his children dandelion salad.

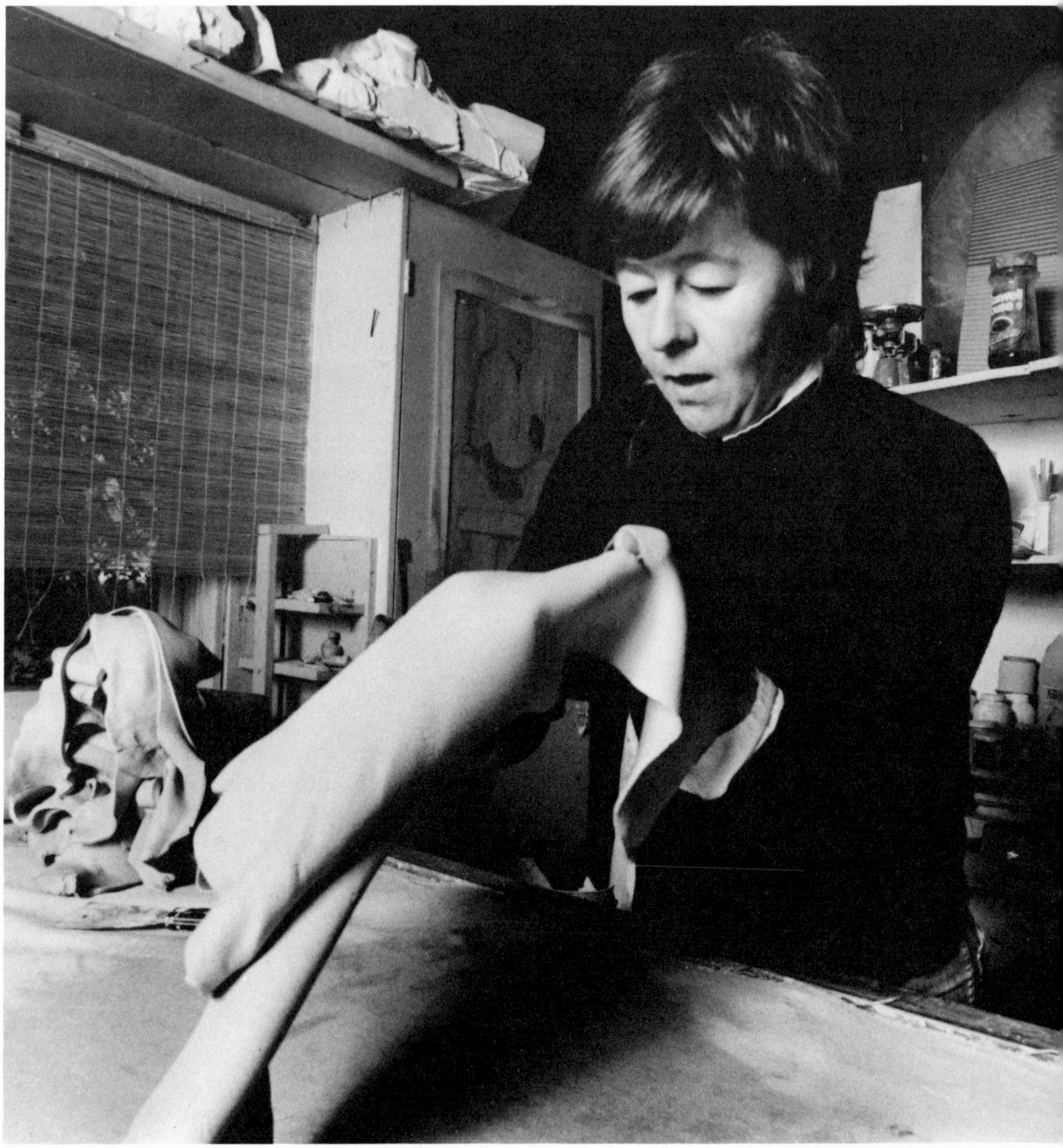

Annemarie Schmid Esler

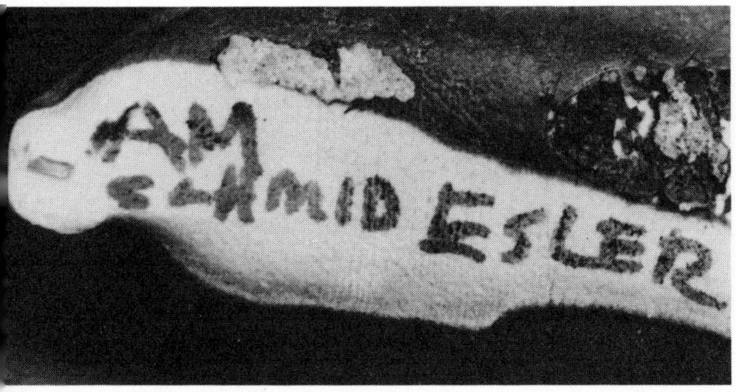

"I was the eldest in my family so I spent a lot of time with my father. I've grown to appreciate the influence he had on me more as I grow older. We had a lot of freedom and not very much structure. We didn't have many material things and we had to improvise our amusements, but we never were bored. I was always interested in drawing, and at age twelve I went to Saturday morning classes at the Winnipeg School of Art. At the art lessons we had the regular staff of the school for teachers. We were seated in the proper light and taught to paint. It was serious stuff. I didn't feel I was just doing something in my spare time; I remember that it was something important to me.

But it wasn't until years later that I discovered clay. I had my BA and had been in Europe for two years, then came back to Winnipeg and got a job as a social worker to earn money for art school. I found the work very difficult, so I looked for some extracurricular activity and I signed up for an evening class in ceramics at the Manitoba School of Art with Ron Burke.

I became very enthusiastic and worked very hard. It was totally therapeutic and I was making very free, very organic things. All my energies were poured into them. I was very naive. If I had had any art education I would have immediately hidden them and been totally embarrassed. At the end of that session I was offered a scholarship for the Haystack pottery school in Maine.

Around this time I also met my husband and we were married. A couple of weeks later I set off for Haystack on the train. I remember coming to a northern Ontario town. I looked out of the window and saw this long platform. I left the train, went over to the other side of the platform and went back to Winnipeg. When I got there my husband was just in the process of packing all our worldly possessions into a U-haul (he had accepted a teaching job in Calgary), so together we picked up the rest of our belongings, got in the Volkswagen and drove to Alberta.

When we arrived in Calgary he taught at the art school. I had investigated other art schools, but since we were in Calgary I enroled in the art school there, taking the regular program in printmaking and painting. But every evening I would work in the ceramics studio. In my final year I took clay as a regular course and we had a very competitive lively class; in fact, most of the people in that class have continued to work in clay. It was a very healthy, constructive environment. We all helped each other, and we didn't have a course to follow. I remember once my instructor remarked, "You always seem to approach everything backwards." I didn't follow what he considered a logical process.

Annemarie Schmid Esler

Annemarie Schmid Esler

My idea was that the concept is the most important thing. I worked hard to overcome the technical difficulties of the material, and I strived for personal expression. I wasn't concerned with 'truth to material' which was a concern among ceramists at the time.

Both of my sons were born during the time I was at art school. It made for a difficult schedule, but we managed with help. Once we built our house and moved out here to live it was easier. I had the garage to work in. At that time I was doing mostly functional work in reduction stoneware. I was trying to support a studio so we had sales for three years. Although the pieces were functional they were a bit sculptural in the sense that I changed them after they came off the wheel. I just couldn't leave them alone. I really appreciate people who throw well. I never wanted to do it; to me a wheel is only a tool.

Raising children and working as an artist is difficult. I find when I give workshops there is a terrific bonding among women on the issue of having children and working as artists. For one thing you have to have an extraordinarily supportive husband because he goes through this whole thing with you – and at times it becomes very difficult. It requires an incredible perseverance and sacrifice, not only for yourself, but for the whole family. I used to feel quite fragmented when the boys were small, but it's not so bad anymore. I think it has something to do with being older and more relaxed. Life is much more comfortable since I turned 40.

When your children are small you never know if it's the right decision to try to keep working. For me it would have been worse to stop working and start again later. With all this energy I have, I am happiest when I am working, and when the work is good it gives me confidence to go on.

The kind of support I get from my husband is hard to articulate – he doesn't talk to me about my work, but he helps make it possible to *do* my work steadily, and that is important.

In the beginning I did functional work just to pay my bills, but now after ten years I feel less pressure because my work, the work I like to do, is moving. It is being accepted more.

I go to a lot of exhibitions, and not just ceramics. I like to see work that has some life to it. There is a lot of dead boring work around, many things that are rehashed. I can't see working in a history in which you are not living. I can identify with people who are curious and working within their own environment. Now I've learned to blank out a lot of what I see and be very selective. As far as my own work is concerned I am pleased when it communicates to some people. Obviously no one is given a guideline as to what to see. They read into it whatever they bring to it, so I am not surprised at what is said or written about my work. But it is interesting that people have so many different feelings about it.

The landscape around here influences me, but whatever is around me influences me as well. For a while I was doing clay collages because I had such a surplus of clay and broken things and old pieces. I cleaned up the studio and made everything into constructions of some sort. It's hard to define exactly what causes a new series of work. For the crow series, for instance, there are a lot of magpies around here, but what really got it started was that I was with the boys in a sports shop in Seattle and in the gun department there was a big plastic crow that hunters use for a decoy. So I bought it and brought it home. It lay for three months in the back of the car, and eventually I took it out, made a mold and cast it. The bird had a compelling, almost mystical presence that moved me very much, so I made more. That's how the crow series started. It's never like grabbing something out of thin air. And then after I start something it becomes more complex, or turns in a different direction. Then I continue working with the idea till I find I'm not challenged any more.

When I work my idea is to present a concept. I'm using the crows to express thoughts about being enclosed – the difference between the enclosed things and the space the enclosure creates. Absurdity, chance and humour also creep into the work. Generally speaking I use what is the most straightforward material. I work very quickly, and I don't like to leave the idea through all sorts of processes. The clay I'm working with now dries very quickly so I don't need a damp room. I just make the piece, put it on the table, dry it, glaze parts of it before firing, put it in the kiln, turn up the kiln fast, and just go through the whole process quickly while the idea remains fresh.

If I find a commercial clay which works well I use it because the process of making clay and glaze doesn't interest me. I did it when I worked in stoneware, but working with whiteware I'm more concerned with the surface, the canvas quality. I was working with porcelain because of its white surface, but found it couldn't take the kind of stress I put to clay. Earthenware can. It's kind of a romantic notion to dig clay – OK on a holiday perhaps – but as far as working is concerned I am interested in the piece I am working on and I just want the materials to be there as cheaply and efficiently as possible. I use commercial glazes too. They are foolproof; they've had a lot of research go into them.

Annemarie Schmid Esler

Annemarie Schmid Esler

What I find most exciting is the process, the involvement with making the piece. Ceramics is very complex. Once a piece is finished it has a special quality and can be a completed piece of art. Then you bisque it, and suddenly it becomes hard and changes again. Then it is glazed and refired and it takes on another dimension. There are three individual statements and they are all valid. I find this enormously challenging and difficult. I don't test glazes much. I usually sacrifice a piece instead of making a test. I like the process of directly working on a piece, instead of testing. At least it is a satisfying experience even if it doesn't turn out well. I end up with many discards this way, but it forces me to re-think the process. But sometimes if I'm working on a new series mistakes are worth it because good things may come out of trusting to chance or intuition, rather than following a calculated plan.

I've always believed that the technical aspects of working in clay shouldn't overpower your work. If you have an idea in your head you will learn the technology. If you get bogged down in a virtuoso display of technology, the work may become impersonal and merely decorative.

I am not a romantic about clay. I am a romantic person in other aspects, but I can't think of anything harder than working with clay, though I enjoy it. If the work is good it is a means of saying things that are deeply personal, things that I couldn't communicate in any other way.

John Chalke

John Chalke has a file folder thick with clippings of magazine reviews, personal articles, and announcements of international ceramic exhibits, one-man shows and innumerable awards. Hidden amongst the glowing commentary about his work is a scrap of paper on which he has a handwritten note: "I make pots, but not because I like to. I make pots not because I don't like to. I think it happens because on some days it feels like a comfortable way out of somewhere . . . ."

Born in Gloucestershire, England in 1940, John received his art training and Teacher's Certificate in Art Education at the Bath Academy of Art in 1961. He moved to Calgary in 1968. His years in Canada have seen many changes and some difficult times–a marriage that didn't work, teaching jobs that didn't last, and desperate times spent digging drains in Vancouver when life lost all meaning. With a move to Edmonton and a return to teaching design, his life became centred again on clay. He has made three trips to Japan to study wood-firing techniques and has travelled to Turkey and Persia to rummage through old kiln sites and dig for shards.

He lives now near downtown Calgary in an old wooden farmhouse that is a pleasant memento of the past in a city overtaken by the cement and steel of modern growth. His studio is a converted garage behind the house. Things that interest him run the gamut from ancient Japanese and Korean pottery to contemporary rock 'n roll. Above all, he has a deep-rooted fascination for the late sixties. He came to Canada with romantic notions of wild frontiers and still plays out that fantasy by dressing as a cowboy. He likes names. His studio is 'The Wild Rose Pottery', named for the clay which comes from a Saskatchewan valley where wild roses grow. He calls himself a 'mud 'n water rock 'n roller' or 'Captain Kickwheel', depending on his mood.

Like the man, his pots are not always easy to understand. In recent years he has been best known for his plates or wall plaques which are multi-fired and metamorphic in character. They combine sensitivity with masculine strength, traditional influences with more obscure counter-culture references, and precise control with the element of chance that is part of the firing process. These large plates are often torn, twisted and stamped with textural details. Like any intricate work of art, they demand close examination.

He works hard to create strong impressions. Even with his more delicate molded shallow bowls, he fires them again and again until 'the feeling is right' and he is comfortable with the piece.

Probably more than any other Canadian potter, John's achievements in clay have gained international acclaim. He is listed in *Who's Who in American Art* and the *Dictionary of International Biography*, examples of his work are published in eight books on contemporary ceramics, and his pots are in private collections in England, the USA, Canada, Australia, New Zealand, Japan, France and Italy.

John Chalke

"I never intended to become a potter. I was trained as a painter – abstract expressionist – in England. But then I got thrown out of art school. It was one of those strange misunderstandings that seem to happen to me all the time. A group of the art students used to go and draw in this Georgian mansion. It was surrounded by a beautiful landscaped garden – trees, mist, lakes – very Italian looking, and I remember once I was so intent on my drawing that I didn't notice that all the others had left. Suddenly it was dark and I was there all alone among these Tintorettos and Rembrandts and I was locked in. I opened a window and jumped out. I remember landing in a rosebed and looking up to see the principal of the school staring down at me. It looked like I was misbehaving and I wasn't, but he threw me out of the school.

I didn't know what to do then, so I got a map out and stuck a pin into it at a place called Leek. It turned out that this was right near a whole area called the Potteries around Stoke-on-Trent. So I learned about clay right there. If I hadn't been thrown out of art school I would have most likely carried on as a painter.

I really got started with no direction of my own. I used to believe that somebody tells you what to do – your mother, or teacher, or the system – but that's not always true. What you have to understand is that when a sign comes from another direction you have to be hip to it, you have to realize it is a sign.

I ended up going back to the college and finishing my degree, but by then I was very much into clay. I illegally lowered a large electric kiln into my basement and whenever the landlord came by I'd throw a blanket over it and pretend it wasn't mine. I remember the first pot I took into a show in London. It was at the British Craft Centre. Ruth Duckworth was one of the jurors and this piece of mine – it was handbuilt – was virtually still warm from the kiln. But it was a good piece and I was pleased with it. Ruth looked up and smiled and said, "It is all right." I'll never forget that.

I handbuilt a lot in those days because I wasn't that good at throwing. There weren't that many potters then in England, perhaps 30 in all the British Isles. I developed a reputation as a sort of individualist. I wanted to do things that nobody else was doing. I became recognized not so much for the quality of the work, but because it was so different. I got invited to more and more shows. For a few years I taught at the Farnham School of Art in Surrey with John Reeve. The school was full of potters and I could work on my own. It was a happy time.

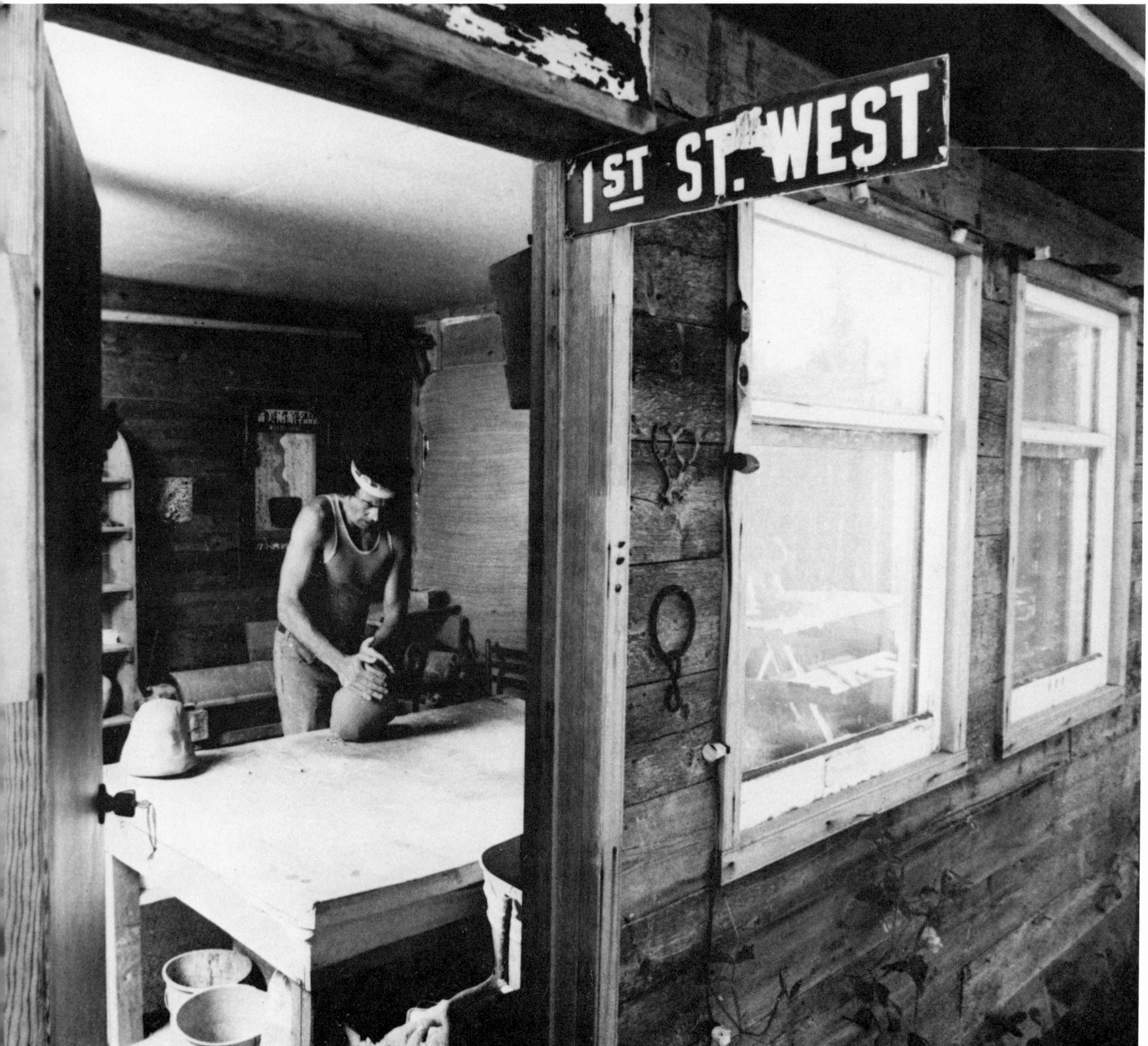
1ST ST. WEST

John Chalke

John Chalke

I decided to come to Canada one day when the rain was beating on the window of the local library and I was reading the Times supplementary section and came across an ad for a job in Calgary. It was for a 'professor' of ceramics. I was impressed. Professor is a term used for 'dons' at Oxford. So I applied for the job. Then one day, right out of the movies, something came from Western Union. I couldn't believe it. Anyway, I got the job and little did I know that the prototype of Canada which I had in my mind was the very place I was going to. I had this vision of lumberjacks, somebody called Pierre with a patch over his eye and an axe over his shoulder...cowboy land!

When I was first here in Calgary I was doing a lot of raku. I really don't know how I got interested in it, but I did develop a lot of raku techniques, built kilns everywhere and wrote several articles on it. I actually got typecast as a raku person.

I've always been interested in wood-firing kilns and had wanted to go to Japan to study their techniques for years. When I was really at my lowest point in Vancouver, penniless and unemployed, I got a registered letter from the post office with a cheque from the Canada Council – a travel grant to Japan. I couldn't believe it. I couldn't go. I was in no shape. But I did go the next year.

The interest in Japan began in England. Potters in England are very influenced by Bernard Leach's teaching and his Japanese experience. I studied old wood-firing kilns. The two kinds of Japanese pottery I like best are Shinoware and Oribe, both seventeenth century.

I've been to Japan three times now and spent a lot of the time studying wood firing. For a long time I was really into it. There weren't any other kilns as far as I was concerned. Now there's much more written about it. It is a lot of work, a lot of chopping and sweating, and it takes skill to get it up to temperature. There are many difficulties, like keeping the wood dry and not stoking too much. It's a lot of looking and listening. You can hear the kiln as well as see the cone. You have to recognize the noises. The kiln talks to you.

I haven't been doing any wood firing lately, but I'm planning to go back to it since I've bought a piece of land about 80 miles northwest of Calgary, a very isolated spot near the foothills. I'd like to build an underground kiln there like the anagama kiln in Japan. I planned all this when I was unemployed in Vancouver. I defined the kiln space. It will be an inefficient kiln so there will be great variety. I like that. All kilns here fire so evenly it's boring. I hope my kiln will fire a little unevenly. People will think I've failed at kilnbuilding.

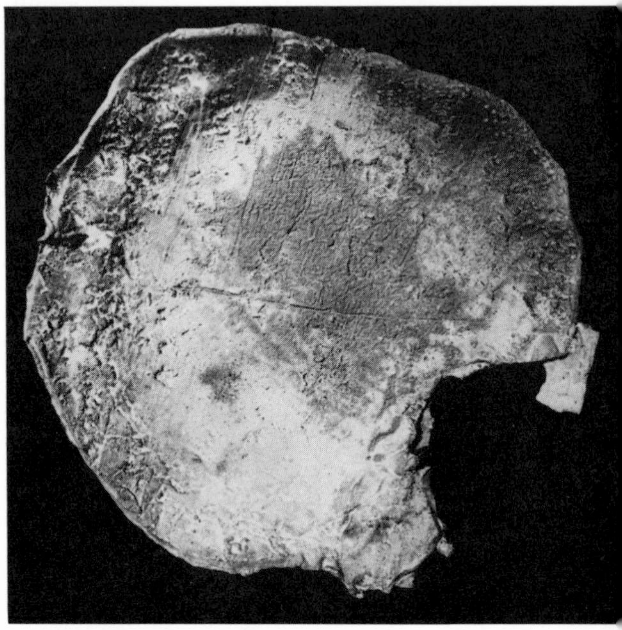

They won't understand.

The clay I'm using right now is great. It's a dark clay and is almost identical to a clay used in Bizen, Japan. If I put a bit of sand into it it's almost the same. Some of the things that are special about Bizen and other traditional Japanese ware are the uncontrolled elements – the assymmetries, the kiln accidents, the vagaries of fly ash – all the things people say are very Zen. I find this very interesting. I don't always have a direction because that would be too definite, too final. I've just realized in the last few years that there is no right or wrong. It is all growing to another stage. I guess if I have a direction it is simply to continue growing.

I'm working at cone 6 now and I can get any colour I want and any texture. But I'm bored with that. I keep adding and firing and then firing again, sometimes eleven or twelve times. I have to fire lower and lower and am even starting to work with half cones now. I always alter commercial lustres by firing them at a different temperature. If it says on the label 'fire at cone 018', I never do. The same thing with the decals. I cut them up, change them, overfire them or something. I have to change it from 'their' statement and make it mine. Sometimes a plate will come out of the kiln after only one firing and I will think it's all right, but I'm always very suspicious of it.

John Chalke

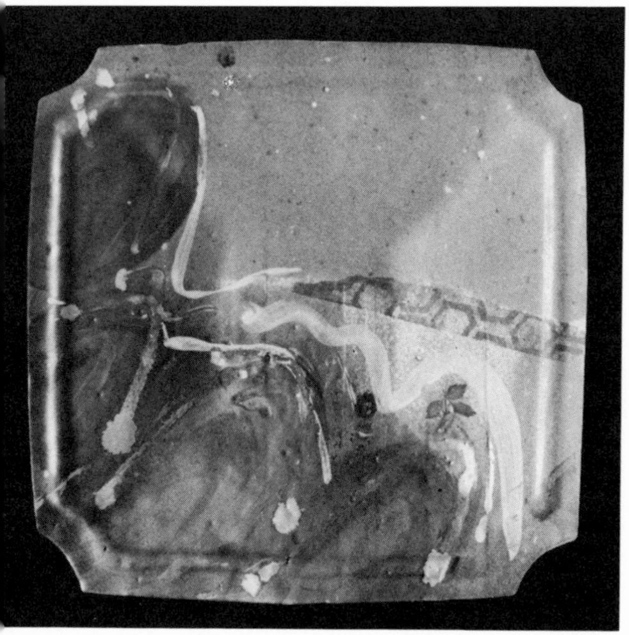

There's a dichotomy in my work and in myself, I guess. I think I am perversely enjoying it. It gives me pain. I make traditional references. I'm very interested in roots. But at the same time there are many counter-culture attractions for me. The rock and roll world is very much part of my life – the music, the sixties, the dope culture. I find these things very hard to share. Most potters are not interested in these things. People think of rock and roll as a simple thing, but it is not. It is very complex, very rich. My head is somewhere back in the sixties and this provides a lot of distractions for me. But I always keep coming back to clay. It is one thing I'm very romantic about.

I'm not very good about sales. I used to think it would damage my integrity if I became commercial about my work, but last year I took a big step and had a sale right here in my house and it was great. I sell now to a couple of craft shops and occasionally people come to the house to buy. I don't keep records of sales. All of the exhibits that I've been in have been by invitation. I don't go after things like that.

I'm not very fond of doing workshops. I usually show slides because the way I work is very hard to demonstrate. It is so much of the moment that when I demonstrate, it embarrasses me. I feel very vulnerable, like people are looking into my soul. It's sort of like being in the zoo, but at the same time there is an exhilaration about it.

I don't think my work has changed that much over the years. There has been a consistency. There's been no dramatic chasm opening up under my feet. My work is rather accumulative of ideas. I know my work for other people is very complex, but for me it is just a logical accumulation of influences. I'm surprisingly more consistent than I seem, which gives me some pleasure, but only in retrospect.

My work habits are unpredictable. My first main discipline in the morning is to make myself a cup of tea and feed the cat. Then I go from there. When I open the door to my studio there may be twenty different things in my mind that I want to do. I talk to myself and to the cat. (Nobody says birds are crazy because they talk to themselves.)

If I wasn't teaching I guess I would have to change my ideas about being commercial. I couldn't afford to do the kind of work I'm doing right now. Maybe this will change and crafts like pottery will demand bigger prices. A lot of people say pottery is not really craft, it is fine art. I think that's nonsense. Of course it's craft. It's just not the same craft as in the days when you had your kick wheel and a rainbarrel at your side."

Jack Sures

Jack Sures

"Living in the middle of the Canadian prairies creates a psychological need to fill the empty spaces." These are the words of Jack Sures who lives in Regina, Saskatchewan and makes voluptuous looking pots to satisfy this need. His work bears no relation to the stark prairie environment and, in fact, seems a planned contrast to the flat harshness of his surroundings. Jack makes pots that are warm and rounded and sensual, like the curved form of the human body.

His reputation as a unique and energetic potter has spread throughout this country ever since he started his first studio in Winnipeg in 1962. At that time he was the only professional potter in Manitoba, and in setting up his studio he built a 30 cubic foot gas kiln, three kick wheels, an electric wheel made out of a discarded milk separater, glaze bins and shelving, all with the borrowed sum of $2000 and *without* the benefit of any formal training in ceramics.

He has lived for fifteen years in Regina, where he is professor of ceramics in the Visual Arts Department of the University. The home that he shares with his family is a few minutes from campus. He works at the school, finding the time between teaching commitments to pursue his own creative ventures in clay. He also found time recently to create and construct a massive 2900 square foot clay mural for the Sturdy-Stone provincial office building in Saskatoon.

He is confident of his talent. He relies on his own imagination to breed new ideas without much outside influence, yet *his* influence has been felt by almost everyone involved with clay in Canada and in other countries as well. Travel grants and sabbatical leaves have enabled him to study and work in Japan, Grenada and France, and his pottery has been shown in exhibitions in many different parts of the world.

Jack's work is a blending of the whimsical meanderings of his mind and the voluptuous qualities of clay. The fairy-tale feeling of these pieces provokes both an emotional response and an awareness of the sheer fun that goes into their making. The fact that Jack is completely self-taught as a potter and that his training was in painting and printmaking has given him a different attitude to clay. His attachments are not to the Oriental or Leach traditions, but rather to the Flemish masters like Bosch, the German Expressionists, the Dadaists and the American Expressionists. Although he respects the formal traditions, his continuing concern is to move beyond the traditional nature of his craft.

Jack Sures

"I find it very difficult for a person to express himself with a pot in a straight formal way. It requires something else. Either you manipulate the clay past the point where it is recognizable as somebody else's, or you do something to the surface. For instance, I hate the 'vertical lathe' look so I rarely leave something just as it comes off the wheel, though sometimes I do if I am going to decorate the surface. A plate which can be pretty simple and boring is a nice surface on which to draw. If I just put an ordinary glaze on it, anybody could have done it. It's not personal.

I think it's important to be an individual in your work without going beyond the respect for your materials. I don't believe in being different for the sake of being different, but I do believe in expressing yourself as much as you can. The leaning aspect to some of my pots is getting away from the vertical lathe again. People see everything in this world as straight down the road and turn right at the next corner. Everything we look at is related to gravity. We even think up and down. Wouldn't it be nice if we could walk down a street and see everything leaning in a different direction?

Everything I do is a self-portrait; my pots all have fat bellies. I like the organic, the voluptuous quality of clay. The way clay folds, bends and creases is like female forms with thighs coming together. All the animals in my work are me. You have to understand my psyche to appreciate what the animals are. You could say, "Oh, it's an anteater," then that becomes the end of it without further looking. If I don't say what it is then you have to think a little bit more about it. It's like people who go to an art gallery and say "Oh gee, there's a barn just like the one we used to have." Then it becomes an identifiable image and they don't experience the painting or the hidden content. A work of art has an objective content and an emotional content. Kids can deal with these things better because they can appreciate them on a more fundamental level than can adults who have too many built-in prejudices.

The fantasy in my work goes back to my original training in painting. I think that making purely functional things puts a strong limitation on what you do in terms of fantasy. Like my teapots. They have gone way past the point of looking ordinary, but they are still functional. Once you have the lid off it pours all right. I always think if people don't like my work at least they can use it! I don't always make functional things, though. I made a whole series of wall plaques in 1975 which I bisqued and then painted with acrylics and oils. They were all either low relief, and built on from that, or inlaid flat pieces. I painted the inlaid shapes and then, after the paint was dry, I took a thick wash

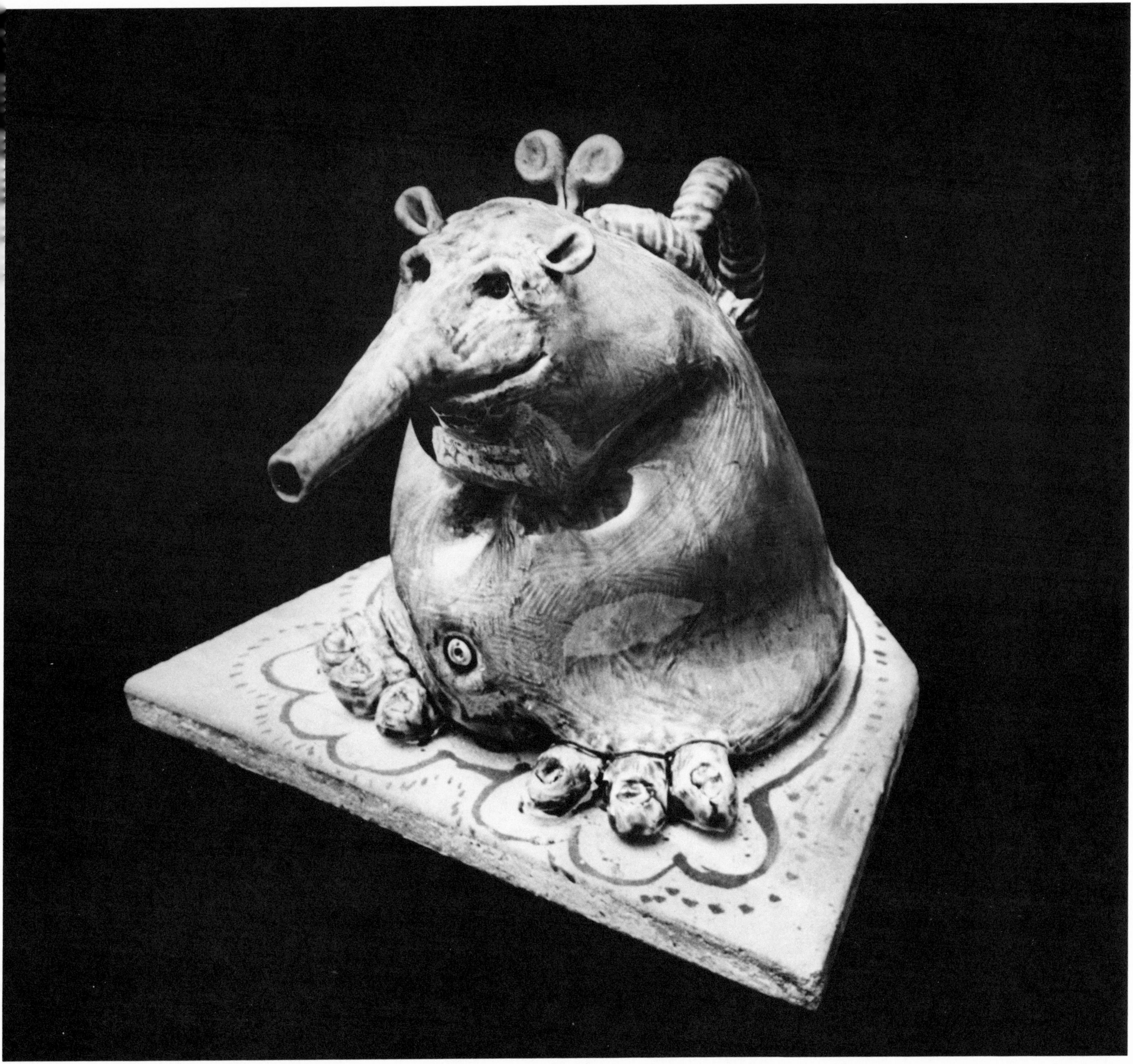

of oil paint and put it all over it. It would sink into all the cracks and then I'd wipe it off and just the fine lines would remain. I used this technique for some cylindrical pieces, but I did glaze them afterwards because they were functional and could be used as vases.

Throwing and handbuilding, 'putting things together', give me the most pleasure. Throwing because it can be soothing and an escape. I enjoy the feeling of activity, the feeling of the form which is created by the activity. I like pieces best before they are leather hard, when they still have that rich clay quality. Glazing is just something that will hopefully enhance the piece. And then the finished work is always anticlimatic. I like the feeling of the pencil, but only in relation to what the pencil is saying. Once I start drawing on the pots it just happens. It all just comes as I go along.

I didn't really enjoy doing that big mural in Saskatoon. It was too long a period of not being creative. Once the idea was conceived and the molds made, it was a straight reproduction. It took 13 months to make and 6 weeks to install. It was like being a potter who sits in his studio and makes 100 mugs a week and 20 casseroles or whatever every day for 13 months. It was just too repetitive. I'm not saying it's wrong to be like that, but for me it isn't satisfying.

My attachment to clay is very physical, but the physical activity also gives me an emotional release. I don't have a romantic attachment to being a potter. I wouldn't jump off a bridge if I couldn't work with clay ever again. I find it is the best for my creative activities at the moment. I find it necessary, but I don't have any great mystique about it. If some people want to wear out the ball joint in their hip because they feel a wheel has to be kicked and they use only a kick wheel, that's fine for them. I don't feel that makes a better potter. I have dug my own clay in the past, but I don't see any advantage to it. It doesn't improve the final product. It's not what you use, it is how you use it that is of primary importance.

I believe there is nothing new in clay. Anything which might appear to be new is a personal way of expressing things which have already been done. In throwing there are limitations and clay has a physical structure that you can't ignore. But the nice thing is that you never finish learning as long as you are developing yourself. Learning is an inside influence. I don't think we've changed much from primitive times. We have different techniques for dealing with society – things we have to cope with – but I don't think we're much different emotionally now than we were 2000 years ago. I can relate

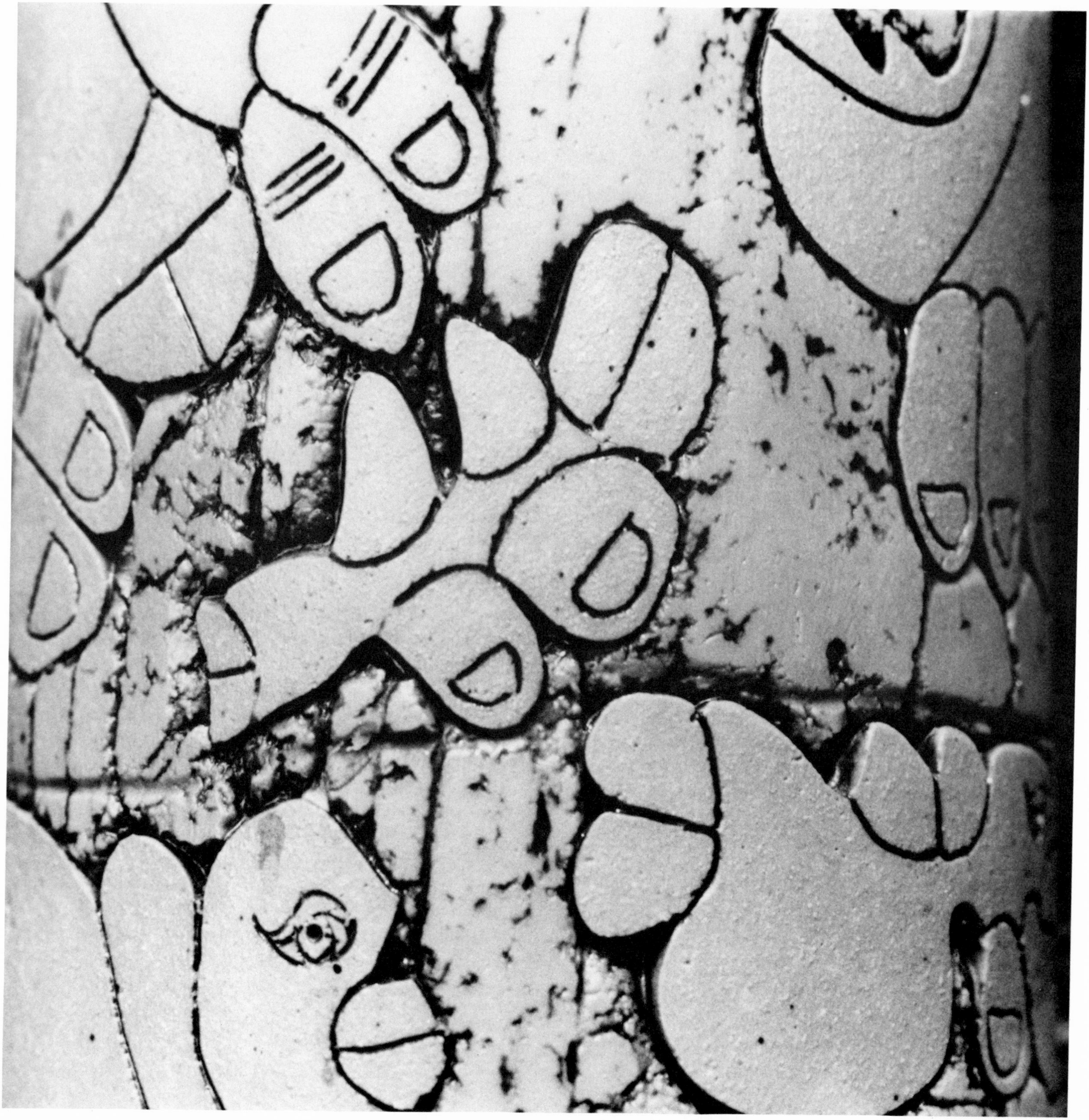

very easily to pre-Columbian ceramics and feel an attachment to the individual who made a piece. I think I can feel the kind of things he was feeling although the content of his society was different. I really don't think there is much emotional difference between him and me as individuals working in clay.

I went to Japan on a Canada Council grant in 1966 and this had more influence on me when I came back than while I was there. There was something about their attitude and the formal aspect of their work that filtered through to me later. Over there, in order to be a respected potter it is not enough to make good pots. One must be of a certain age and experience. I didn't recognize the truth of that then, but I do now. I think one essentially changes and hopefully gets better. My attitudes are growing and I have a better understanding of what I am doing now. When I started with clay I really didn't understand it. It takes time. Sometimes people can make unique statements but – and I don't want to sound pompous – art school kids, though they may have interesting ideas, can't honestly express themselves in their material to the best advantage of both, simply because they haven't had enough experience to understand their individuality.

I think part of the maturing process is understanding oneself better. Before, I always had to be creative in the sense of making new things all the time. I didn't take time to get into things deeply enough. I did a lot of bad things simply because I didn't develop them all the way. Now that I am older I am a little more respectful of what I am doing and I take more time. The only thing I worry about is growing stale and repeating myself. Technically you reach a point when you can say what you want to say. But to be able to go beyond that to say something unique about yourself, that's tough!

Living in the middle of the prairies in a small place like Regina has disadvantages. I don't see much of what is happening in the craft world. I miss seeing shows and exhibitions. Some people come here and they hate it. I've been here since 1965 and I'm learning to appreciate it more and more – the subtle changes, the dramatic changes, and especially the big empty spaces. I think it affects my work too. You have these empty spaces that you feel you have to fill, somehow, psychologically. It certainly makes you conscious of yourself. If you ever get out in the big fields and for three hundred miles all you can see is wheat and flat prairie, it makes you feel a bit insignificant. But there's a freedom about it. You can go in any direction. If I had to live elsewhere I guess I'd like to live on the seaside, but then the prairies are a little like the sea. There is a feeling of limitless space, and the sound of the wheatfields rustling in the wind is akin to the sounds of the sea. There's a feeling of emptiness out here. Maybe I'm trying to fill it. Maybe I'm trying to prove something to myself."

Keith Campbell

Keith Campbell

There is nothing slapdash or haphazard in Keith Campbell's pots. Precise control and painstakingly long hours go into every piece of porcelain that he produces. Every detail is carefully executed down to the last golden tendril. This same sort of precision and planning is seen in Keith's approach to life. Operating on what he calls 'five-year cycles', he has come a long way in thirty-two years.

There was little in his background to foster an interest in pottery except his own love of art. When the 'Woolworth mentality' of his native Niagara Falls started seeping into his consciousness, he abandoned that city and moved to Toronto to study at the Sheridan College of Design. After graduation, teaching positions led him to George Brown College in Toronto where, as head of the Ceramics Department, he instituted the college's entire program. On cue, after five years, he left to embark on his next life cycle, which was to buy land, have his own studio, and start a family. All of this has now taken place in the home in Northern Ontario that he shares with his wife Terry and baby daughter Alexandra.

Since 1973 Keith has worked entirely in porcelain. He uses the pure white luminescent quality of this clay body as a white canvas background for the lyrical images he creates. He relies on one transparent glaze and decorates with stains, oxides and lustres. Anywhere from eight hours to four days may be spent on a single piece. The demands of porcelain are such that breakage and warpage take a large toll and once, in frustration, after losing some favorite pieces in a lustre firing, Keith sat down and calculated his income to be about $1.85 an hour.

He works in a studio at the back of his house looking out on 100 acres of rugged bush, beaver ponds and pre-Cambrian rock. The adjacent highway leads to North Bay, where he is a teaching master at Canadore College. The land is rough and rocky, but there is a well-worn path back to the beaver pond trodden down by Keith and his dog. These harsh surroundings seem somehow at odds with the delicate lustre decorated porcelain that is the hallmark of this young potter. Changes take time and influences creep in gradually. Just now the overbearing presence of the land is beginning to show in his work. In Keith's latest airbrushed plates, gray rock faces loom starkly against the pure white porcelain, combining the roughness of the land with the pristine quality of this potter's art.

Keith Campbell

"I think living up here in the bush has influenced me. The airbrushed plates are certainly a change in my style that reflects my surroundings. But I'm doing it gradually. It's difficult because once you develop a style people expect that to continue. You can't just throw something new onto the market. I'm trying to be more versatile instead of just doing totally lustre or overglaze decoration. Using the airbrush gives me a break from lustring as well. It's a different feeling.

Seasons affect my work, too. They are so strong up here. I look out my studio window and am very conscious of them. The winters are long and cold – 45 below zero. It's really bleak and it's hard to get the energy up. It shows in my work. The pieces don't seem to ring as much. But once spring comes I get inspired more often. And then the summers are really beautiful and it's hard to stay inside and work. There are disadvantages to living out here. I don't get to see many exhibitions and I miss that. But the worst thing is getting materials and transporting pieces. I have to drive 250 miles to Toronto to get materials because shipping is so expensive. I had two students who ordered $250 worth of clay and the shipping cost $225.

Everything I make I basically make for myself, psychologically. I make so many pieces that I have to sell them, but I do make each piece to please myself first. It's an ego thing. I've been told that I'm still in my infancy stage because when I make bowls I put little drawings on the inside, so if you're eating your cereal and you come to the bottom there's still something there.

My work schedule changes all the time, but I usually throw four or five pieces at a time and then work on them from there. I like to complete the whole cycle. I don't like having a lot of bisque pieces lying around, because usually each piece is thought out when I start working on it and I want to complete that before it's gone from my head. This method gives variety to your work. You're not just throwing and throwing. You do a little throwing, then some decorating, then loading the kiln, then applying lustre. You mix it up and it makes it more interesting.

There are a lot of potters who do really beautiful loose things which they dip, or they throw the glaze on or they splatter. But that's not me. Before I started working in porcelain I was using stoneware and being constantly frustrated because I was trying to make porcelain-type pieces, trying to do porcelain decoration on stoneware. I was just learning then and I wasn't quite sure of what I wanted to do, but I thought it was

important to focus on one thing. So I focused on porcelain and got more and more into decoration.

My wife says that I'm really a frustrated painter because I use the pot as a canvas to paint on. I've always been interested in decoration, but in the beginning I was very inhibited. I used to draw everything on paper first. Now I draw directly on the plate. It's almost second nature. All my drawings used to be contained in a circle, but now I'm branching out. It's all related to freedom from inhibition.

My students are inhibited. As soon as they start doing something and people start watching them they feel that they are being judged. I encourage them to see the work of as many potters as possible and then try to make those kinds of pots. When I graduated from Sheridan I made pots that resembled those of Jack Sures, Vivika Heino and Bob Held. They say it takes you five years to work that out of your system. I didn't believe it, but it was five years after I left college that I really started to develop a style.

There aren't many people doing the kind of work that I do because it's just too tense, for one thing. The materials are very expensive; there are too many firings; and it takes so long. Just applying the lustre on one teapot can take about eight hours. It takes me so long because I decorate all parts of the pot, even inside the foot of a bowl. This is a very important part of my work. It gives the piece another dimension; it seeps through to the other side. I like to think that whoever is washing the dishes will still get a thrill when they turn it over.

The materials I work with are very expensive, so I'm trying to cut my costs by firing at a lower temperature. I'm firing at both cone 10 and cone 6. I use the same clay body and some of the pieces aren't totally vitrified at cone 6, but since they're mainly decorative and not used for cooking it's not so important. The interesting thing is you can't tell the difference in the pieces. I think a lot of potters will start firing at lower temperatures because of the energy crisis.

I'm doing more throwing than handbuilding right now, mainly because of time limitations. But I love handbuilding. I think it's the more creative part of working with clay, although throwing has a magical quality about it. I can remember when I first went to Sheridan College to do furniture design. I had to take ceramics as one of my courses and the first time I saw someone throwing on a wheel I was so inspired. I'm still enthralled by the throwing process. It is magical.

Keith Campbell

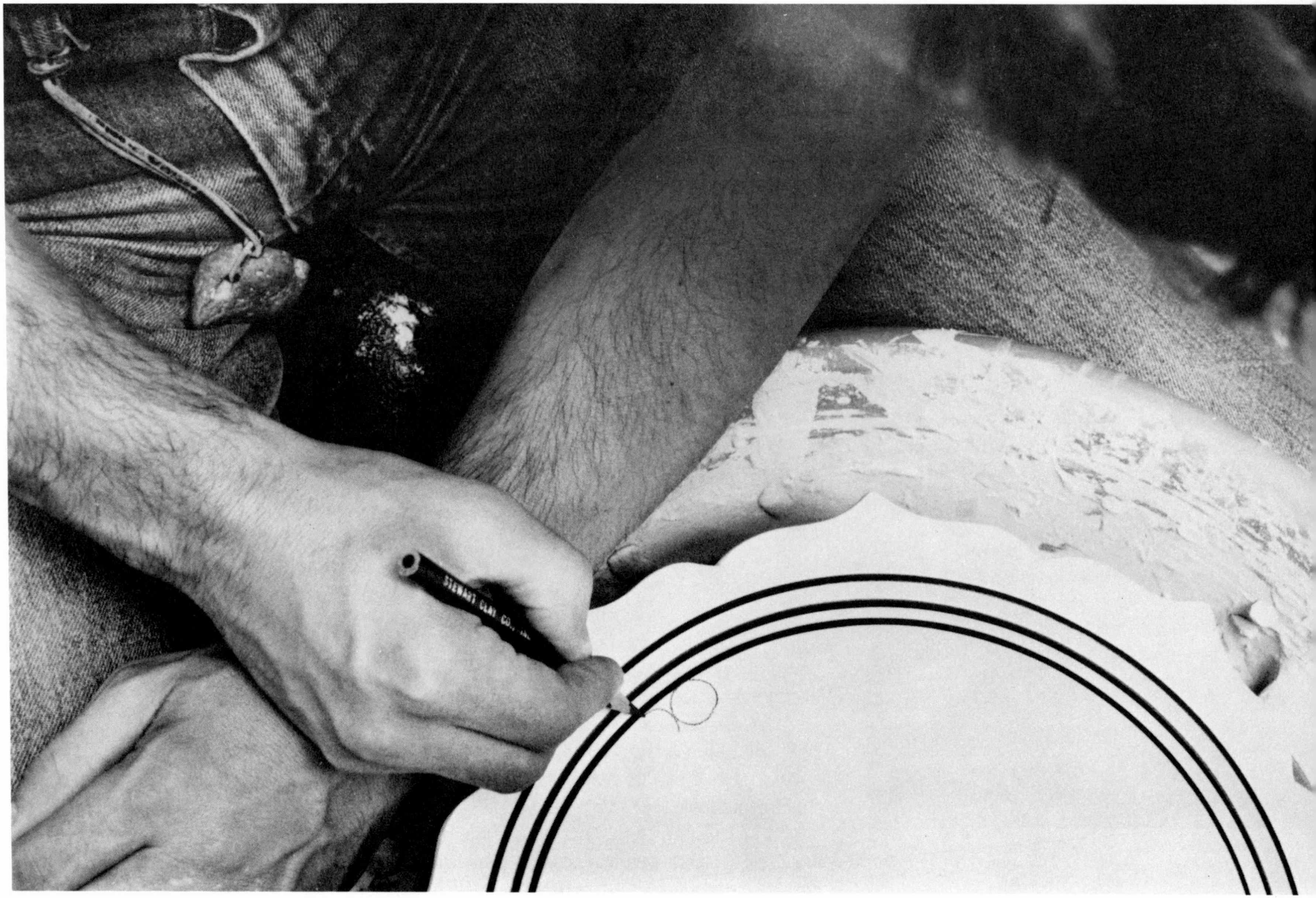

Keith Campbell

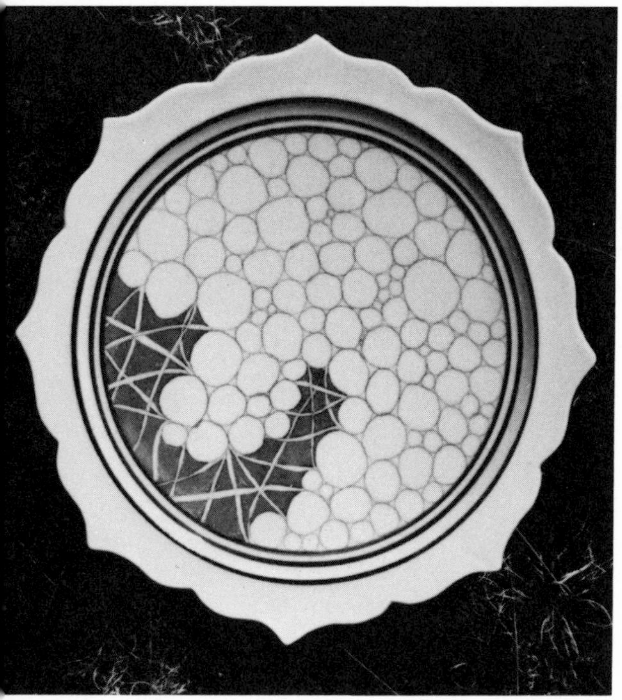

Keith Campbell

I can't imagine ever wanting to stop doing pottery. There are so many things to be done. I've been in pottery since 1967 and I'm still amazed at the number of things to be experienced. It takes years and years to learn just one thing. People don't understand that. Students come in and if there are ten glazes they'll use every one once and then think they've done it all. In Japan they work on one glaze and one clay for ten years to find out what it really has. I just use one clay body and one glaze right now – a transparent glaze and a porcelain clay body. And then I use stains and oxides and lustres, but that's it.

I think there is a lot of fantastic work being done in this country right now. But the problem with Canadians is they don't think other Canadians are valid until they're accepted by other countries. There should be better organization in this country for craftsmen to enter international shows. For things to happen here I think it's important that we all pull together. I try to be involved with organizations, conferences, jurying shows, that sort of thing. Giving workshops is another good way to spread more information about the craft. I do quite a lot of them.

I think of my craft as my whole living experience – my house, my studio, my profession are all the same thing for me. Whether I'm refinishing a piece of furniture or working on a pot, I put the same kind of emphasis on it. Being a potter is very fulfilling. It's ego, in a way. I can look at a piece that I've made and say that it is me in a lot of respects. You can see a resemblance between a potter and his work. My work is very clean, concise and orderly, and this reflects me. I'm very controlled and my work is very controlled. I never leave anything to kiln accidents. I know exactly what's going to come out of the kiln and I like that kind of control.

I don't think that I have that much talent. I just think that I have an ability to work really, really hard. It's the only way to become good. The ones I remember at college who were really talented went nowhere. The trouble was that it came easy to them and they didn't have to work. I think that successful potters are very hard workers. You can't do it any other way."

Jack & Lorraine Herman

At a crossroads outside Kleinburg, Ontario stands a colourful house cluttered with handicrafts and crackling with the diverse personalities of Jack and Lorraine Herman, two of Ontario's most established potters. They fight, they laugh, they finish each other's sentences and they survive after twenty years of living and working together.

The original building on their one-acre property was an old wood frame schoolhouse now converted to a studio where these two potters work side by side. The family home was built beside the studio when the Hermans' two children were small. Now they have grown and left home, and Jack and Lorraine stay on amidst the comfort of their own pots and a growing assortment of artifacts collected in their travels to far corners of the world.

In the late fifties when the Hermans began their career as potters, they were like pioneers in the field. Almost entirely self-taught, they learned by their own and each other's mistakes. Right from the beginning their styles have been different, and they both consider this a positive factor in their survival as a team.

Jack throws earthy stoneware pots and Lorraine handbuilds delicate porcelain figures. Between the two of them they have won countless awards and developed a legendary reputation over the years. They still put in long hours in the schoolhouse studio, but it is easier today than it was in the early days.

Jack & Lorraine Herman

Lorraine: After Jack and I met I went to England and worked with a potter for many years and then when I came back we got married. He was in the restaurant business then and I had no idea he was going to go into pottery. I'd have run in the other direction so fast if I'd known.

Jack: Our first studio was in Bolton...

Lorraine: ...in the basement!

Jack: It was a terrible time. We had no money, no booze and we lived on sausages. Lorraine won't eat them to this day. What made it so hard was that we had little training and there were no schools in Toronto, no one to turn to for help. I finally got fed up, dropped everything and went to Alfred University in New York State. I became more confident after that. It opened my eyes to what pottery should be for the first time. I should have gone long before.

Lorraine: We both worked long hours in that cold basement. Jack worked eighteen hours a day and we had two small babies at the time. I can still remember them standing at the top of the basement stairs howling and I always felt guilty. It was horrible. Potters shouldn't be allowed to have children.

Jack: There wasn't a big market in those days. I used to decorate everything within an inch of its life in order to sell it. And we had to sell it in order to eat. We'd go to the stores and flog it ourselves.

Lorraine: Once one or the other of us won an award then it was OK, it got better. Of course, it was easier to win the prizes in those days. I used to win first prize for ceramic sculpture at the CNE and there'd only be one other lady (*lady* you notice) competing. It didn't mean you were any good, but at that time I needed that little pat on the back.

Jack: Professional potters were considered to be very strange people in Bolton in the fifties ...

Lorraine: ...and I thought we were very respectable! I remember once they were going to have a 'beatnik' dance at the high school and half the class came to the door at one time or another to borrow either something to wear or a slim volume of poetry. Jack had a beard and I didn't know what euchre *was*, much less how to play it! I felt very cut off; as if I was living in a separate planet all by myself.

As time passed life became easier, their reputations grew and the move from Bolton to the Kleinburg schoolhouse gave them space and incentive to carry on. Jack's style is consistent and distinctive. He makes wheel-thrown country pottery – casseroles, vases, platters, mugs, kitchen and table wares. He works with stoneware which he fires to reduction in a large gas kiln. His pots are sturdy yet elegant with subtle decorative touches.

Jack & Lorraine Herman

Jack: It's important for a potter to have an identity so that people will know and recognize your work. You have to know your strong points and what kind of work suits you. For instance, I worked in porcelain for a while and now I hate it. I don't even want to touch it. I finally faced the fact that porcelain isn't me. I like the stronger forms you can do with stoneware. Mine is country pottery, simple earthy pots that could be from any country.

I think there are different levels that people work in and one of them is physical, the force that you apply to your material. There's an excitement in having something you can attack. The other way to keep going is by becoming interested in little things that entice you. I amuse myself by saying I'm going to make the ultimate bean pot. It's a game that I play with myself. And then, of course, I make fifty bean pots and I hate them all because I haven't found the one I want. But that's the fun!

I don't think I've changed that much in the last twenty years. Slight changes, maybe. I do less production work. I just make whatever I'm thinking of at the moment. Right now I'm interested in doing more ash glazes. I started about a year ago and gradually my pots are getting more and more dismal looking. No colour, just ashes. This obviously is going to lead me to be interested in woodfiring kilns, which is something I want to do before I drop dead. I like to have that timeless quality about a pot. As I get older I'm leaning toward simpler and simpler pots and simple glazes and shapes. By the time I'm 95 they won't even exist! The more subtle I get, the harder it is for me to sell. Who's going to give me $50 for this dirty grey pot that I think is beautiful?

It takes a lot of searching to find out why one chooses a profession like this. You certainly don't do it for the money! There may be a hereditary factor. My father was a tailor, so I grew up with someone who was working with his hands and enjoying it. I was also very impressed with the idea of working on your own. I could never work for anybody else. I only did once, when I was eighteen. I hated it so much I walked out and went to California and I've never worked for anyone since.

I know that in two or three years from now I'll still be making pottery, but I can see myself doing less. I don't feel it absolutely necessary to be making a pot as the last thing in your life, to die at your wheel and all that. I'm not getting tired of it, but I think you wake up and realize there's another world besides staying home and working on your wheel. I've sometimes had 'potter's fatigue' where I just get sick of it and I go away for three or four months. I think this is a syndrome that many potters encounter. It often comes after a long period of overworking.

Jack & Lorraine Herman

Jack & Lorraine Herman

Lorraine works primarily in porcelain, creating delicate figures and intricately decorative handbuilt boxes and planters. Her figures are often whimsical characters that reflect her laconic sense of humour. She is more interested in creating with clay than in the more technical aspects of firing and glazing.

Lorraine: My things are all fired with Jack's and I use his glazes. I don't know anything about glazes. Often I combine them in a strange way because I don't know any better and sometimes I get a good result, sometimes not. I do so little that I couldn't have a separate firing. It would take me the rest of my life to fill a kiln!

When I was in England I started by decorating a potter's plates. Then I began fooling around with the clay. I made a lot of little piggies, about a gross a day. And I became hooked. What I know about clay is using it, that's all. I don't know anything else.

Porcelain is very very nice to work with. You can make all sorts of twiddly things if that's the way your mind works. I like fiddling around. I sit and smooth something to make it neat even when it will never be seen. It must be something like knitting. It soothes me; I like doing it. Then I put a glaze on it and even if it's a thin glaze all that smoothing effort is covered up. But that's the way I work. I try and stop myself now and then, but it doesn't work.

I started out studying illustration and that has affected my work. I figure all my pieces look good maybe from the front and maybe from the back, but they hardly exist at all from the side because they are still illustrations. They're not sculptural. You really can't look at them from all different angles. I've always been interested in costume design and that led to making a lot of figures in costumes as authentic as I could make them without using draped lace. I haven't done any of them lately because the last few had such mean faces that I couldn't stand it. And nobody noticed but me.

When I first started doing figures I did a lot of madonnas and mother and child things. I thought people had to have a *reason* to buy my work. I slowly eased out of that and then when I was in my thirties I did elegant dribbly ladies. There's something significant that I'm now doing older people. Changes in my work are slow and ideas creep up on me unexpectedly. I'd like to be stricken with inspiration a little more often. I sit waiting for it and nothing happens. I sometimes think that all the young people who do exciting things must have a clever idea at least twice a week.

On the whole my work is getting smaller and smaller. A lot of the time it is small because I like my work desk messy and, as the mess encroaches, the work space becomes very tiny and I have to do little tiny things. I'd love to make big loose things. That's why I like to go to Mexico. I work in such a tight way and they make marvellous big things so casually and the effect is terrific.

Jack & Lorraine Herman

In recent years travel has become an important part of the Hermans' life. They live and work together, but never travel together. Jack loves to hitchhike through different parts of the world, while Lorraine heads for South America or Mexico, boards a bus and goes where it goes. She'll often sit alone for hours in a distant market square just watching, or sometimes sketching, the people who gather there. After more than twenty years of living, working and raising two children together, they need this time away – and alone.

Jack & Lorraine Herman

Lorraine: We're probably the only couple who have survived together as potters. It's a very hard thing to handle working and living together twenty-four hours a day. One thing that helps is we don't have any professional jealousy between us because our work is so different.

Jack: We have a lot of admiration for each other's work and we separate frequently. We have separate friends, separate interests, and we're not jealous or dependent on each other.

Lorraine: Ladies often come up to me and gush and say how wonderful it must be working with your husband. And I think, "Are you kidding?"

Jack: Despite what Lorraine just said, I must add that it is a good feeling and an advantage to be working with someone whose taste and professional standards are equal to yours and who is sympathetic to what you are trying to do."

Wayne Ngan

Walter Ostrom

John Chalke

Lorraine Herman

Tim Worthington & Pam Birdsall

Gaétan Beaudin

Monique Bourbonnais Ferron

Byron Johnstad

Ruth Gowdy McKinley

For most potters the creative and physical challenge is in the forming process – the molding of clay from a lifeless lump into an object of beauty. For Ruth McKinley the commitment to form is equalled, perhaps surpassed, by her commitment to the firing process. She has been firing with wood for twenty years and it is this difficult, time-consuming and physically demanding process that provides for her the complete harmony of being a potter.

Wood-firing kilns are not readily available to many potters because fire regulations prevent their use in most urban areas. Ruth is fortunate to live on the campus of Sheridan College, School of Crafts and Design, in Mississauga, Ontario where she is permitted to fire her wood kiln. She lives there with her husband Don, the Furniture Master at the college, and their twelve-year-old daughter Lauren. As resident potter Ruth has a gentlemen's agreement that she will be available to the ceramic students at the college.

About once every two months, when Ruth is firing her kiln, the great gushes of black smoke sifting throughout the campus are a dramatic symbol of the excitement and intensity involved in the process. It takes from 22 to 24 hours to complete a firing, which means that Ruth is up most of the night watching the kiln, chopping wood and listening for the distinctive quiet which means that it is time to stoke again. It is this intimacy with the kiln and the firing process that continues to delight her and to demand her respect.

Respect for this material called clay in all of its aspects, from the powdered form in which she buys it to the fire that finally forms it, is apparent in Ruth's work. She works slowly and gives so much thought to the line and form of each pot that her husband claims she remembers every pot she's ever made.

As a child growing up on Long Island, New York she studied classical piano with the ambition of becoming a concert pianist. It was only by chance that her path was diverted. She accompanied a friend to Alfred University and ended up spending six years there, graduating with a Master of Fine Arts degree in ceramics.

Ruth Gowdy McKinley

Ruth Gowdy McKinley

"In 1949 I entered the New York State College of Ceramics at Alfred University. I knew very little about clay and ceramics, but during the following years I was fortunate in studying with Charles Harder, Marion Fosdick, Clara Nelson, Clarence Merritt and Daniel Rhodes. Alfred certainly provided a good grounding for me in the ways and means of potting.

The skills and knowledge I gained there, and the beginnings of a personal direction for my work, were all tested when I worked at the Ossipee Pottery in New Hampshire with two friends, both former Alfred students.

I was developing a repertoire much like a musician who studies and practices the music of various composers until understanding and mastery of the works are achieved and the performing of them is as natural as breathing. A potter also has to explore, experiment and practice with the various methods of forming clay and the varying temperatures at which different clays and glazes mature. Once you have all the techniques, machines, tools and experience, then you can work with certain harmony because of that knowledge.

In working with both stoneware and porcelain clay bodies the potting vocabulary is extended for me. The rugged nature of stoneware clay suggests a simple and direct spontaneity in throwing and building. Porcelain is more refined and finicky and demands more exacting and disciplined control – a restrained spontaneity – in the throwing or forming.

The decision whether to use decoration, texture, engobe, slip or glaze is often made while I am sketching or during the forming of a pot. I attempt more and more to view the piece as a whole and finished work as I'm initiating it in my mind.

There have been intervals in my life when potting was not possible. The most recent period was in the late 70's when I wasn't physically able to throw on the wheel. I concentrated more on sketching. I became aware as I was sketching that I was also perceiving the clay and the forming almost as if I were throwing. I could actually feel the clay and the wheel. This responsive sense has remained. Now I not only do some sketching prior to throwing but frequently, while involved in throwing a series, I will stop to note the form changes I see possible for the next pot in that series. Always, the *next* pot will be better.

Ruth Gowdy McKinley

For me, as with most potters, the potting process begins with a concept and the ceramic materials at hand – the many types of clays, feldspars and quartz. I have great respect for these materials. After all, many were formed eons ago in gigantic and tumultuous upheavals of fire, water and wind, and my respect for them is only equalled by wondering at my audacity in presuming to wet, work and fire them yet again! Possibly this feeling for the materials was a factor in my choice of wood firing. I must be as involved with the firing as with the forming. As I form the ware I also form with the fire.

All firing alters the ware, but my pots fired unsaggered in the down-draft, wood-burning kiln have an additional alteration. During the firing, wood ash is deposited on the ware throughout the pot chamber. When you reach high temperatures (2360°F or 1290°C) the ash melts and fuses with the glaze, engobe or with the clay of the pot. After all these years I am still in awe of this firing process, although the variable effects are becoming more predictable and planned for, both in the designing of the ware and its placement in the kiln. Each time I stack I try to remember previous firings, remember the locations within the pot chamber where ash deposits were heavier or where the flames, in licking through the bag wall, left strong encircling and flashing patterns on the pot. There are certain glazes which are right for particular ware of mine, although one or two are not as happy with a lot of ash fusing with them because they tend to craze and their appearance and textural quality are altered. These pieces I stack in areas where little or no ash reaches.

The ware is quite literally out of sight in the kiln for a total of 2½ days. The firing cycle is 24 hours and the cooling cycle is 36. I can think of no other endeavour where the work is so removed from the maker's view for so long a time while such incredible changes take place. A piece that appeared glazed purple will emerge a satin black and another that was pink upon loading into the kiln will be revealed as any of several browns, golds or greens with surfaces ranging from dry matt through semi-matt to shiny and transparent.

I have always made functional pots and my concerns have been to consider the form with the function. In all aspects of living I believe beauty and use should be considered equally. If it is a teapot, first it must look good, otherwise no one would pick it up to discover if it performs well or not. Some works promise much and perform not at all. I know I have made them at various times. The forms slowly change as perspectives shift and insights sharpen. The return to previously explored form themes is just one of the many cycles within cycles. Sometimes I feel there are great leaps forward, even leaps

Ruth Gowdy McKinley

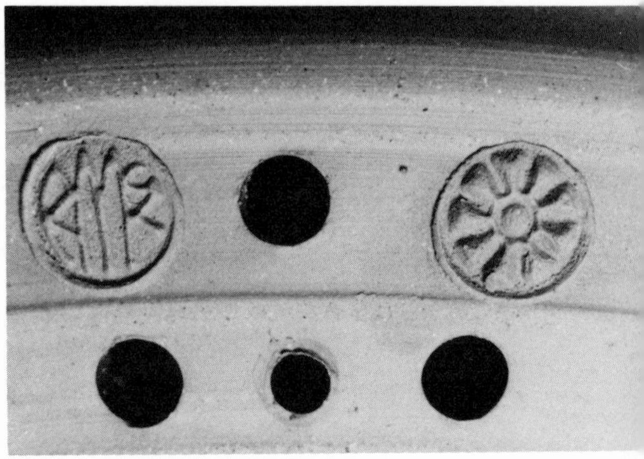

backward, but for the most part the increments are only fractions of an inch. Yet I don't feel limited or restrained. I often think of the piano. It has only 88 keys, but the musical combinations have not been exhausted. Sometimes I find myself thinking that to have total freedom would be to have the greatest limitation.

I work very slowly. I've tried to be faster but I simply can't do it. I am just not a plastic, spontaneous potter. The colanders I make are an example of how finicky I am. The holes in them are not just holes; they are all countersunk so that there is a bevel on the edge of each hole. I drill the holes by hand first with a drill bit and then, when the pot is dry, I use a woodworking tool to countersink every one of them. It's very fussy and time-consuming but, in a way, it is just part of me to do that. I think it is a part of the respect that I have for clay that I can't just poke a hole in it.

There are no short cuts of any lasting value, no instant success formula. As is any endeavour of significance, it's an ongoing process of change and development, a constant re-examination of one's aims and goals. A rich and full repertoire alone is not a substitute for the imagination. I believe that creativity can and does expand, because the disciplines experienced and learned will free the heart and hand to work in concert with the head."

Ruth Gowdy McKinley

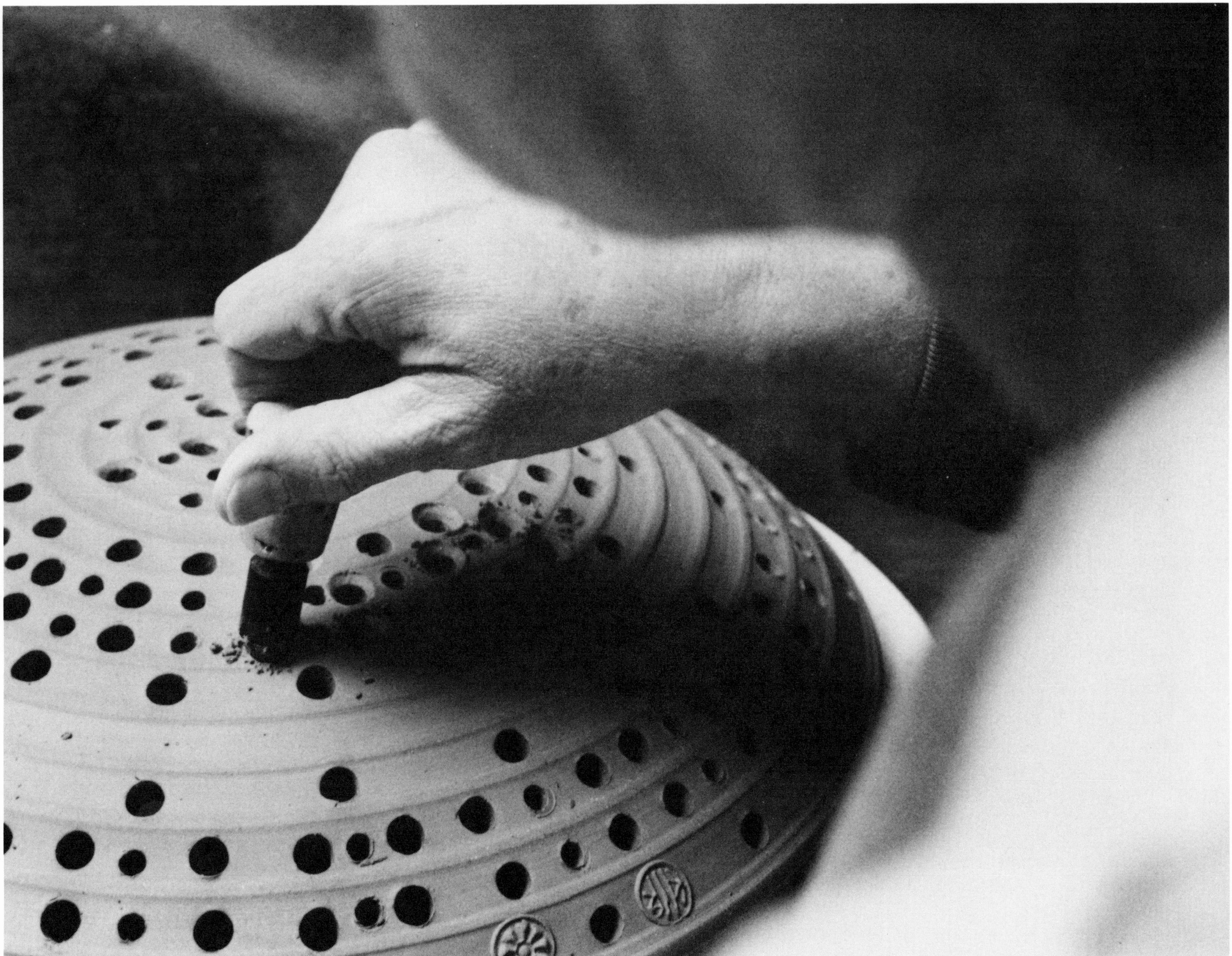

Roger Kerslake

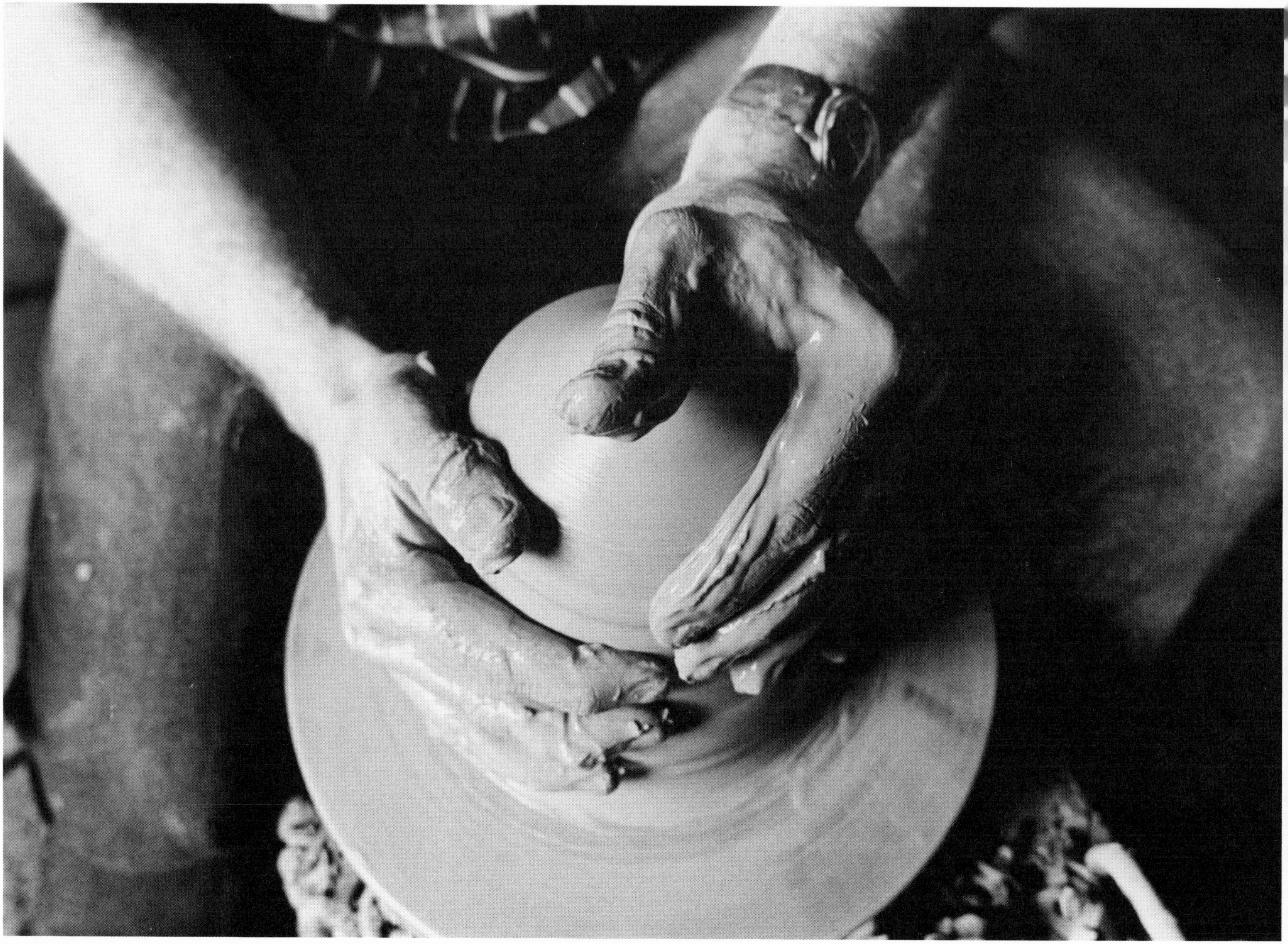

Roger Kerslake

Horseshoe Valley Road stretches like a tapering ribbon through the hills and farmland north of Barrie, Ontario. At the edge of this road a gingerbread-trimmed farmhouse looks like many others except for a sign which proclaims it the 'Studio Pottery of Roger and Heather Kerslake'. Roger bought the rambling house because the adjacent barn had the potential to become a working studio and showroom. Years of scraping, painting and restoring have created a cheerful home, and the barn is now a complete pottery studio with a spacious showroom up in the rafters.

Roger was born in Devon, England in 1938, and first began learning pottery at the Dartington Arts Centre when he was fifteen years old. He went on to study art and design at the local school of art for four years, graduating with a National Diploma in Painting Special. His initial craft training was much in the traditional English-Leach philosophy. A further year at London University with Gordon Baldwin allowed him to combine the potential of clay with his knowledge of drawing and painting.

After teaching and potting in his home vicinity, at thirty he felt that his comfortable existence was inhibiting his potential. So on a bleak day in February, 1970 he arrived in Toronto with his tools and a suitcase.

He was able to find work as a production thrower in the Toronto studio of David Long, then became a ceramics teacher at Central Technical School. Adjustment to the big city was hard. He missed the village atmosphere of Devon, so when the opportunity arose to head the ceramics department at Georgian College in Barrie he accepted. He bought the old farmhouse and moved to the country, back to a slower pace of life quite close to what he left behind in England.

Roger's life revolves around his work as a potter and his teaching at Georgian College. The discipline required to keep the studio running leaves little time for outside interests, and his only release and total escape is playing the trombone with a local jazz band. This camaraderie has become an essential antidote to the solitude of potting.

His wife Heather was once his student and now works with him in the pottery. Her own work is primarily earthenware and raku, but she also helps Roger in the domestic ware production, often with a playpen at her side since the birth of their daughter Devon.

'Journeyman potter' is the term Roger uses to describe himself. He is someone who transforms clay into functional forms in the traditional sense of the village craftsman. The idea that working with clay is in any way spiritual or exotic amuses him and belies the practical attitude with which he approaches his craft.

Roger Kerslake

"I think of what I do as primarily a craft. I have always been more practically oriented. This probably relates to my family which has included cabinet-makers and weavers, though not potters. I guess it's all part of my heritage. The gestation periods required in painting are too formidable. Tactile exploration with clay is more related to the practical need in me to make pots.

I was fifteen when I first knew I wanted to be a potter. My mother started taking pottery classes at Dartington and I looked at these pots she made and thought it looked pretty easy. As it turned out the pottery classes were on Wednesday afternoon which was sports afternoon at my school. I used to feign illness, a sprained wrist or something, to get out of sports and go over to the art centre. I was very lucky that the teacher, Marianne de Trey, was one of Britain's top domestic ware potters and I learned a lot from her.

I think it is unfortunate that we don't have the apprenticeship system here in Canada. In England it was a five-year program and what you did, normally, was pay the potter for the first year and then eventually, as your work improved, the potter started to pay you an appropriate salary until you were ready to start out on your own. I think this is the very best training for anyone who wants to be a studio potter. In school, because of all the equipment and the variety of work, you can develop more of an individuality, but you don't learn the amount of hours that have to be put in or the cycles which full-time potting demands. When you're an apprentice you realize that things have to be finished even if it means working until midnight. There is no such thing as 'nine-to-five' in your own studio.

Eventually I'd like to spend more time working in my studio and less time teaching although I wouldn't want to lose contact with the students altogether. I have the advantage of teaching what I enjoy doing and I think it's important that a teacher should be a practising craftsman. If one is fresh it is easier to pass your ideas on to the students and respond to theirs. But I think that I'm now at the stage in my life where I'm ready to do pottery fulltime. I know the techniques, the rhythms, the processes. I can only do this three months of the year now because of my teaching commitments and I find it takes me a while to get into the rhythms. This cyclical aspect of potting is one thing that is hard

Roger Kerslake

to impress on my students because everything at school is so fragmented. Pots sit around for months without being fired. I'm trying to teach them that in your own studio making pots is only a small part of the whole process.

I am very much in tune with the craft of making and I enjoy making casseroles and teapots just as much as individual handbuilt pieces. I have the financial advantage of teaching and having Heather work with me so I can take the time to explore some new dimensions. I find that I am influenced more by organic things than anything else. Rhythms, movements, surface textures – anything that clay will do can be a starting point to develop a work.

Living here in this small village suits me. I don't like to be pressured at all. I have always had an aptitude of either doing a tremendous amount of work or just ticking over. Hopefully, during the high energy peaks something important to my evolution as a potter will develop. But when I'm at a low energy level I can still keep producing and that's where the domestic ware fits in nicely with my own personal rhythms.

I really enjoy salt glazing because you can arrest more freshness, more feeling in the clay. There is more spontaneity in the making and, for me, less tendency to overwork the pieces. I do the salt glazing at Georgian which is one advantage of being in a school situation. I find that in demonstrating different processes like salt or raku it will often give something different to my work that I wouldn't get if I was just working in porcelain or stoneware. There is a different spirit that comes from the different firing processes.

I am more in tune with the actual practical forms, the surfaces and enrichment of the pot itself, than with glazing or technical things. For about eight years I didn't use glazes at all. The important thing for me then was to explore forms and surface textures and I just used oxides instead of glazes. I think that very often, unless you have a really super glaze, you can detract from, or lessen the form.

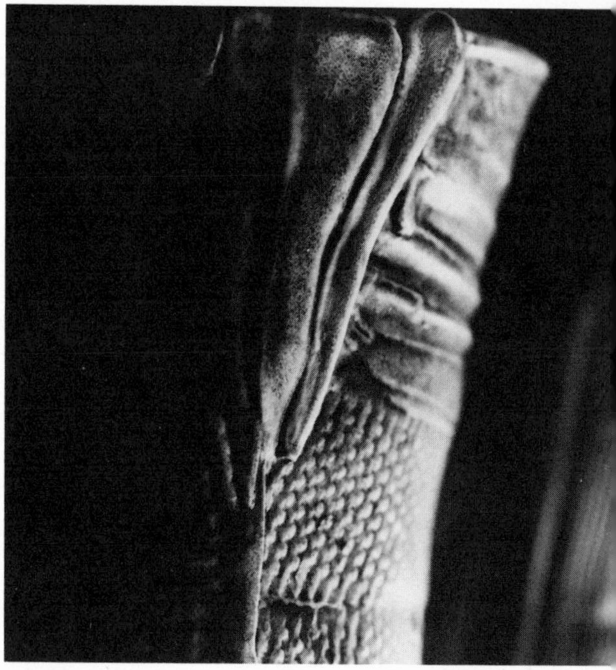

I tend to get bored with seeing the same things all the time and try to move in different directions. Lately I've been trying to find different ways of applying handles. I'm using an extruder to form the handles and then sometimes altering them when I attach them to the pot.

The most enjoyable stage for me is still the making. I hate seeing dry pots around. I don't like bisqued pots because in those intermediate stages the clay has lost its initial movement. It is inert. Making and taking out of the kiln are the great parts. It is an exciting thing to open up a glaze kiln, even if you have only three pots which are worth the firing.

Roger Kerslake

Roger Kerslake

I'm never frustrated by clay because I know exactly what it will do. The technical expertise is deeply ingrained I guess. For me the frustrations are caused by external things like the clay freezing, finding a glaze bucket skimmed with ice, the phone ringing, anything that interrupts the rhythm of my work.

The joy comes from wanting to get out there and do it again and again. The continuum, and the fact that nothing is ever final. What is happening in clay these days is very exciting. There's been a tremendous artistic upsurge in the past few years and people are just beginning to realize what can be done with the medium. I think it's going to continue and I want to be part of it. Pottery is something I have to do. There is a great need there."

Ann Mortimer

Ann Mortimer

When a potter claims that one of her major interests is organizations, it is not surprising to find that she is president of the Canadian Crafts Council, past president of the Canadian Guild of Potters, co-ordinator for international conferences on ceramics, and a valued spokeswoman for the concerns of artisans in this country. Ann Mortimer is committed to the growth and understanding of crafts, particularly ceramics, in Canada.

This involvement in organizations means travel, correspondence, and a lot of time spent away from her studio; time that she doesn't entirely regret since her aim as a ceramist has never been to become a large volume producer. She prefers to concentrate on individual pieces as developments of particular themes. There is a unique quality of softness in both the colour and form of her work which is particularly evident in her slip-cast porcelain spheres, woven plates and planters.

Ann was first introduced to clay while taking a smocking class at a local craft centre, and when the birth of a second son made her realize the futility of this interest she began gravitating to the ceramics classes. Before long she was hooked on clay but, still regarding it as a hobby, she was unaware of where this affinity would lead her.

Special energies and family co-operation were required to juggle a career as a potter with the demands of running a home and raising children. But Ann managed to do just that, as well as attend Georgian College in Barrie, Ontario as a full-time ceramics student for two years, later returning to that institution as a teacher. Throughout this time she was also becoming increasingly involved in the dreams and plans of the organizations that support crafts.

Many changes have affected Ann's life in the last few years. The most difficult was the sudden death of her husband in 1978 which left her with two teenage sons, the trauma of emotional adjustment, and a need to re-evaluate her life and priorities. At that time she gave up her teaching position at Georgian College and decided to fulfill a longtime dream of building her own home and studio on a remote piece of land near Newmarket, Ontario. Now that both sons are away at university, she lives there alone on a wooded hilltop overlooking a lush valley which provides an everchanging vista from both the house and the studio, which was purposely designed to be bright and sunny after so many years of working in a basement.

Ann's background as a musician, nurse, airline stewardess, wife and mother gave no clues to the twists and turns that were to occur over the years and it is probably due to her eclectic approach to life – a philosophy of opening many doors – that she has become today such a major force in the field of Canadian ceramics.

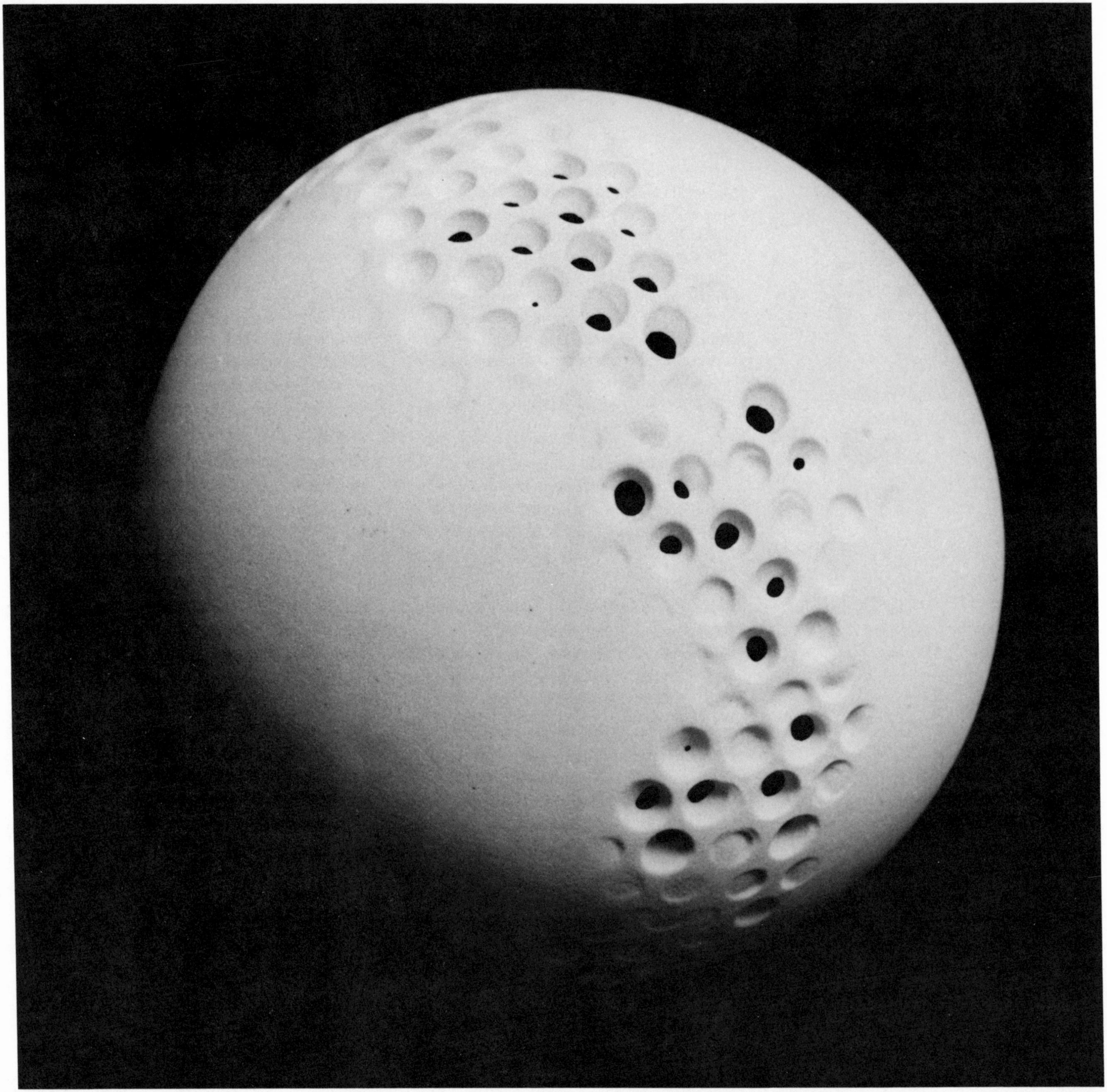

Ann Mortimer

"Like many people, I needed an outlet for self-expression, and for me working with clay was the solution. I was very fortunate in the beginning to have excellent teachers, first Merton Chambers at the Hockley Valley School, who was very patient and helped me overcome that first awkwardness and insecurity of not knowing what I was doing. Then Roman Bartkiw and Ron Roy who both had a tremendous way of dealing with people on an individual basis. I still see Roman's influence in my work. The sandblasted porcelain spheres that I make probably go back to his influence. He often made large voluptuous forms and showed a concern for surface.

Teachers are very important. I always remember a class I took at Kingcrafts Studio in King City, Ontario. A male teacher pointed to a woman who was pressing her fingers down on the edge of the clay and he berated her in front of the entire class, saying that if she wanted to make piecrusts she should go home. It was a destructive and unfortunate statement which greatly embarrassed the student who was just beginning to explore the potential of clay. At the same time, it was a good lesson for me. Later on, when I became a teacher, I remembered that incident and tried never to destroy someone's efforts in a brash or insensitive way. Criticism and observation are important, but there are positive ways in which to get your point across.

I worked for many years when John and Scott were small, in a very fragmented way, but the time came when I wanted to fill great gaps in my background. At this time Robin Hopper was setting up the program at Georgian College and convinced me to enroll as a full-time student. I remember the day I was to start there because I lacked confidence in my abilities to cope with many of the courses. It was really a crazy day. I started to leave the house at 8:30 in the morning and then delayed, kept stopping and starting. I finally got there at 3:30 in the afternoon. The distance travelled was 36 miles!

It was worse than I imagined it would be. It was like undressing in public. I had no background in drawing or art and here were all these art students who had grown up with a pencil in their hand. I positioned my easel in a corner far away from everybody else. I remember the design and colour courses were like entirely new languages for me.

As it turned out I was the only ceramics student who graduated in my year. The younger students resented having to take many of the subjects like history and psychology, so they dropped them in favour of more unsupervised studio time. I didn't waste my energy in rebelling. Instead,I did these subjects because I thought the importance of them might surface later. It was tough for me, but I came from a generation that didn't challenge authority so much. And now I think these studies were worthwhile; they have slipped back into my approach and have demonstrated their validity.

Influences in my work come from many things and are sometimes hard to pinpoint. I took a ceramics history course from Garth Clark in Bennington, Vermont a few years ago and we saw endless slides. I came home absolutely blitzed; the input had been overwhelming. I went north to our island in Muskoka and I remember feeling that I just wanted to get back to something basic, to somehow distill all this stimulation. It was then that I started weaving with clay, a technique that continues to interest me. And yet I can't relate this directly to some slide that I saw in Bennington. I think people nourish themselves in different ways and I find now that I get more, in terms of colour and texture input, from a fibre or photography exhibit than from a clay exhibition.

The environment brings nature to the forefront as a source for form, colour, texture, pattern and the accidental. I have lost the skill to record with a pencil, so my mind and my camera record stimulation for my work. Sculptures of drifted snow are photographed and then, with a rolling pin and a chunk of clay, I try to ease the material into forms that translate my sensitivities. Words and events often buzz in my head. I make quick notes and return to them when I'm in the studio. I did an exhibition piece that was a collection of envelopes, stationery, pens, paperclips and so on – all made from clay, titled 'From The Office Of The President'. This came about when I was teaching at Georgian and also President of the Canadian Guild of Potters and the school wanted an exhibition of the faculty's recent work. All I had been doing that year was writing letters and doing preparation work for the history and chemistry courses, so I did this piece as a play on words for the exhibition.

People grow in different ways. My involvement with organizations creates opportunities to meet many artisans, to view and discuss their work and to learn. Doing is important and I don't deny that, but the many things that I have been exposed to through my travels for organizations and as a workshop leader have flooded my mind and permit me to distill ideas and approaches of importance to me. I refuse to buy the idea that you must turn out copious quantities of something in order to be a legitimate professional in your field. Being considered a professional is a responsibility that you have as an individual for the quality of your work and the integrity with which you approach it. Professionalism doesn't have anything to do with dollars and cents or the volume of work.

Ann Mortimer

I am no longer teaching on a full-time basis and wish to focus my approach. The real problem at Georgian (which was also an opportunity) was that there was a salt kiln and a wood kiln, reduction and oxidation kilns, and raku, so you tended to explore all those processes. I'm now concentrating on two things: raku and a line of handbuilt dinnerware made from a cone 5 clay. I chose to handbuild because my time is still too fragmented to get the fluidity that throwing requires. I'm working on designs with ceramic stains and a clear glaze for the dinnerware.

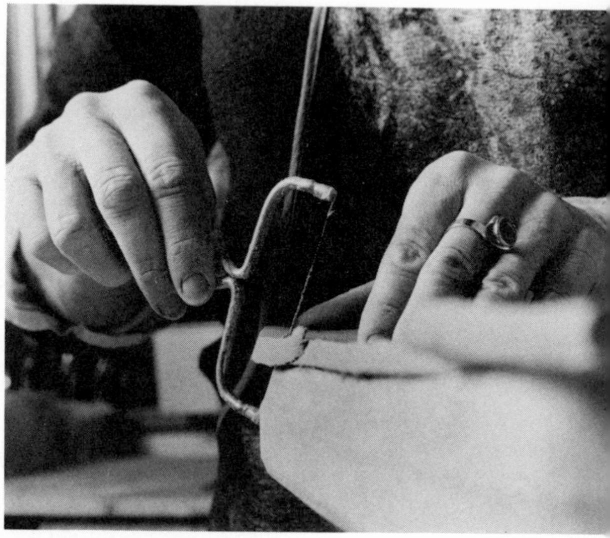

In some ways, the time taken by my involvement with organizations is frustrating. It keeps me from my own work, but I stay involved in order to contribute to, or re-imburse the entire field of crafts, because my life has been enriched by my involvement with clay and with the national and international community of artisans. One of the concerns of the Canadian Crafts Council is that the division between arts and crafts still exists. It is a division of our own making, without historical precedent in many countries of the world. Unfortunately, many people relate crafts to the bazaar type of item produced by hobbyists for fund-raising purposes. We seem to be able to differentiate between the 'Sunday painter' and the professional painter, and we accept that the work of the painter, printmaker and sculptor has a place in our national and provincial, public and commercial galleries. But many galleries and publications continue to deny our best artisans the same public exposure of their work. Works of quality should have such exposure so that the community can recognize the objects and their makers as an important part of our culture.

I have never had what I refer to as 'tunnel vision'. There are potters who establish a direction or a road for themselves and they follow it without veering to the right or the left. They maintain that same focus and don't allow themselves to get side-tracked. My life is more one of opening one door and finding six more on the other side. I go through one or two of those and another half-dozen open. My life has been rich because I've been responsive to the challenge of change."

Ann Mortimer

Gaétan Beaudin

Gaëtan Beaudin

The name of Gaétan Beaudin is as closely linked to the development of pottery in Quebec as the name of Bernard Leach is to pottery in England. Gaétan started as a potter in the 1940's when it was a virtually unknown craft. He became a source of inspiration to a whole generation of Quebec potters who admired his intensity, envied his ingenuity, and learned from his creativity. Today, many of these protégés are aghast at the turn that Gaétan's career has taken. After years of admiring this man's commitment to the craft they cannot understand his current position as the co-founder and designer of Sial Ltd., a company which mass-produces a line of ceramic dinnerware. Gaétan himself says that they treat him like a defrocked priest because, to them, industry represents evil and the craftsman is sublime.

For Gaétan, however, the progression to industrial ceramic design was a normal and natural evolution of his talents. He has always approached pottery in an innovative way seeking new and better solutions and striving to demystify the craft and make it more available to the public. The validity of his concept of a mass-produced line of ceramic ware was confirmed by an exhibition of teapots by Marcel Beaucage, a young Quebec potter. The show was a sell-out and there were dozens of people who wanted a Beaucage teapot but couldn't have one. Gaétan's reaction was, "Why not produce what the public wants?"

Today, the Sial plant in Laval, north of Montreal, employs eighty people, has a capacity of eight hundred dinnerware settings a day, and sells its product throughout Canada and in five European countries. Gaétan is responsible not only for the design of the product, but for the innovation of many new processes and tools used in the plant. He invented a glazing machine that uses different sponge heads to fit the greenware shapes, and then began carving designs in the sponges to create design effects. He developed a method of salt glazing whereby a thin coating of a special sodium compound is applied directly to the pot on the assembly line. For multiple glazing, he constructed a plexiglass holder embedded with hypodermic needles and plastic catheters to control the flow of glaze. The ingenuity of the man is evident in every corner of the Sial plant.

The prospect of continuing forever as a studio potter was too narrow for Gaétan. He needed a larger forum for his ideas, ideas which he claims "are never lonely". Even as a child growing up in a poor family in southern Ontario he showed signs of the entrepreneurial spirit that has continued to forge his adult life.

Gaétan Beaudin

"I've always had this habit of starting things, trying something new. When I was a child, travelling shows of boxers and wrestlers used to come to our small village. The next day I would set up an arena in our backyard and get about twenty-five kids to pay a penny to watch the match. Sometimes I was in the ring breaking a lot of noses, or else I'd match two kids who hated each other so it would be a sincere fight.

I guess I was a bit on the delinquent side as a child. I was not a good student. When I went to the École des Beaux-Arts to study painting and sculpture I finally became settled, discovered ceramics (there was a crude unequipped department there at the time) and began to have some direction. I had a small pottery studio in Montreal before I graduated. It was a very difficult time because there was nowhere to turn for help in 1944.

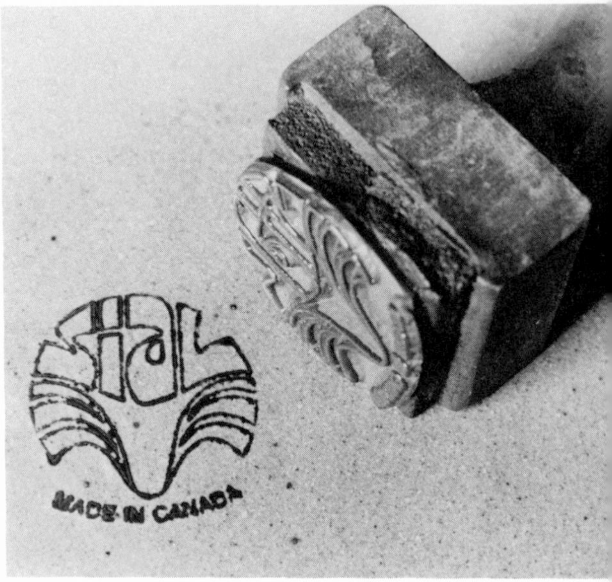

In 1946 I accepted a job teaching ceramics in Rimouski, about 400 miles from Montreal. It was a technical training school and there was lots of money from the federal government because all the veterans were coming back from the war and needed training. I was able to equip the department very well, but the whole idea of having a ceramics department there was premature. The students who came to this school were from parishes all over that region and had been sent to become carpenters, or plumbers or electricians. Often after taking some ceramics classes from me they would go home and tell their parents that they wanted to become a potter. Their parents would say, "What the hell is that? We don't want you to become something we don't understand so you better be an auto mechanic or a carpenter." So they all dropped ceramics and in the eight years that I was at that school I only had three students. It was really a wonderful learning time for me. I did all kinds of experimenting and learning about industrial methods. I even ran a small factory making molded pots at the same time.

During my years in Rimouski I spent three summers teaching at the Penland School of Crafts in North Carolina. I was impressed with the set-up there, with the fact that you could teach for two or three months in the summer and then produce your own work for the rest of the year. So when they closed the department in Rimouski I decided to open a summer school.

It was in 1953 that I found the place in North Hatley that became the summer school. It was an old abandoned hotel, but it was very large and the property was beautiful. It was right on the shore of a lovely lake close to Sherbrooke, Quebec. I fixed up the place a bit and then started having summer courses in three-week sessions. Some of the students stayed for the whole nine weeks and there was room for everyone to live at the school. It was really fun at the beginning.

Gaëtan Beaudin

While I was at North Hatley I continued to do a lot of experimenting. I was the first person to do stoneware in Quebec; it wasn't being done at all at this time. I was sort of a pioneer in terms of stoneware and glazes. All the young potters around used to come to me to get my recipes. And then I was continuing with my own production when I wasn't teaching. Marketing my work was never a problem because the market in Quebec has always been very good. Producing enough was the problem. And then, of course, in the beginning I wasn't competent enough and couldn't avoid making a certain amount of junk. Some people today consider things like those early pots of mine 'primitive', but I don't think in these times that we can be primitive. It is not honest today to be primitive. We are not like characters in novels who can move forward and backward in time.

In 1966 I gave up the school. It got to the point where the students were either complete beginners or people who took up pottery as a hobby, and I was finding it difficult to be an adequate teacher to people who couldn't catch on to centring or wedging. I think that everything in life has a certain rhythm, a start and then a finish. And though it still exists, that was the finish of the school as far as my evolution was concerned.

This was a low point in my life. I was feeling very empty and I was in doubt about myself. There had been a great intensity involved for me to try to prove something, and then I felt I had proved it and didn't know what came next. I was considered a master, I had very successful shows, people bought my pieces and put them on their mantelpieces, but it wasn't at all what I wanted to be. At the same time I was becoming more concerned with social things and politics. I thought that little things mattered more than gathering around the 'golden calf'. I dismissed the idea of becoming what people call an artist because I disagree with the way that artists take something very precious and present it only in a certain way. They lock up beauty in their galleries. They are like priests who lock up Jesus Christ and the only way people can get to see him is to dress up on Sunday and go to church.

With all of these doubts in my head I went to Japan for a year. That destroyed a lot of the myths for me and gave me a different philosophical attitude toward pottery. I came back with a thousand-piece collection of Japanese pots and I opened a small store and sold them all. I guess that proves that I am not attached to anything.

When I came back from Japan I knew that I couldn't carry on in the same way. I just didn't agree with that concept of art being exclusive. I thought of the medieval times and those sculptures, many of them masterpieces, that were made by nameless masons

who didn't sign any of them. They went to the churches and worked on these sculptures, often in teams, with each person expressing his own feelings and dreams. And it was there for everyone to enjoy. I became very preoccupied with all of this, and that's why I went into industry.

In the first stages of Sial we were just making clays and glazes for potters and schools, but it has grown and we have done a lot of industrial experimentation and have developed a lot of new techniques. There was a great challenge in setting this up. In the beginning we had no professionals to draw on – no mold makers, nobody with twenty years of fettling experience. So the product had to be designed to cope with that. My product is constructed so that it goes through one firing; my glazes are compounded so that they work without causing problems of application; we have no handles that have to be added on and no mold made from more than two pieces. We had to adapt to our conditions. And I had to work as a potter to come up with the original designs, sometimes making as many as five dozen of a single item before settling on the right shape or size.

I am convinced that industry can be good or bad, but the fact that I have taken this route does not make me popular with many craftsmen. There are some potters who are quite good today who started with me and related to the way I was then. Perhaps I transmitted to them some sort of intensity. I don't think it was doctrinal, but for them it seems it was almost a religious approach to the craft. Industry is very loathsome to them and now some of them are acting as if I was the Pope and I announced that I discovered the body of Jesus Christ. I think the average potter in Quebec is a very insecure person, economically insecure anyway. And the best way to protect this insecurity is to justify the lack of certain experimental or new things.

I don't miss being a studio potter. I think it's like asking a musician who was a soloist and is now leading an orchestra if he misses being a soloist. I feel more like a conductor and composer. I am not composing directly, but I am just a step or two removed from it. I don't miss being a studio potter, because I am, after all, still a potter."

The Work of the Potter

Roger Kerslake

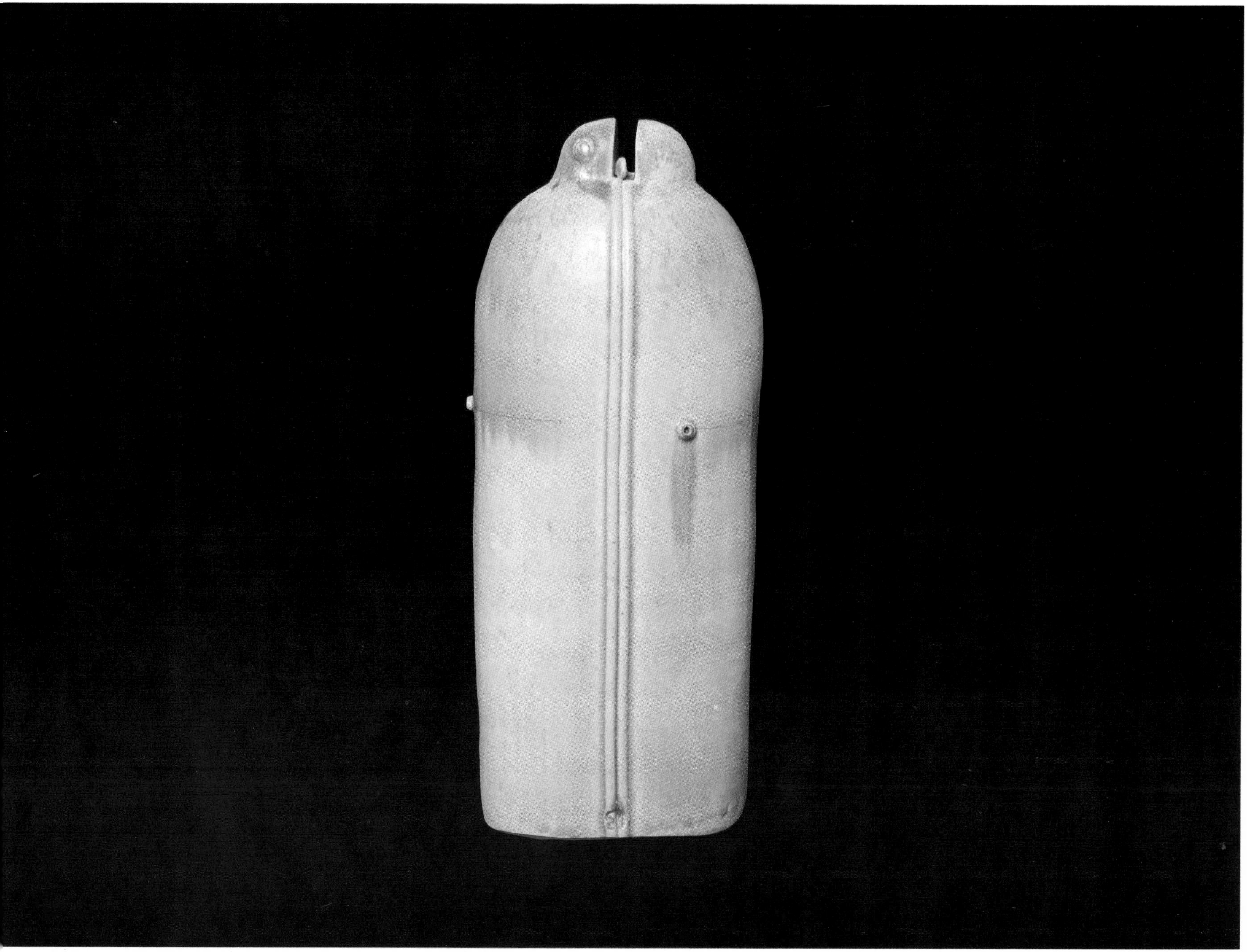

Ruth Gowdy McKinley

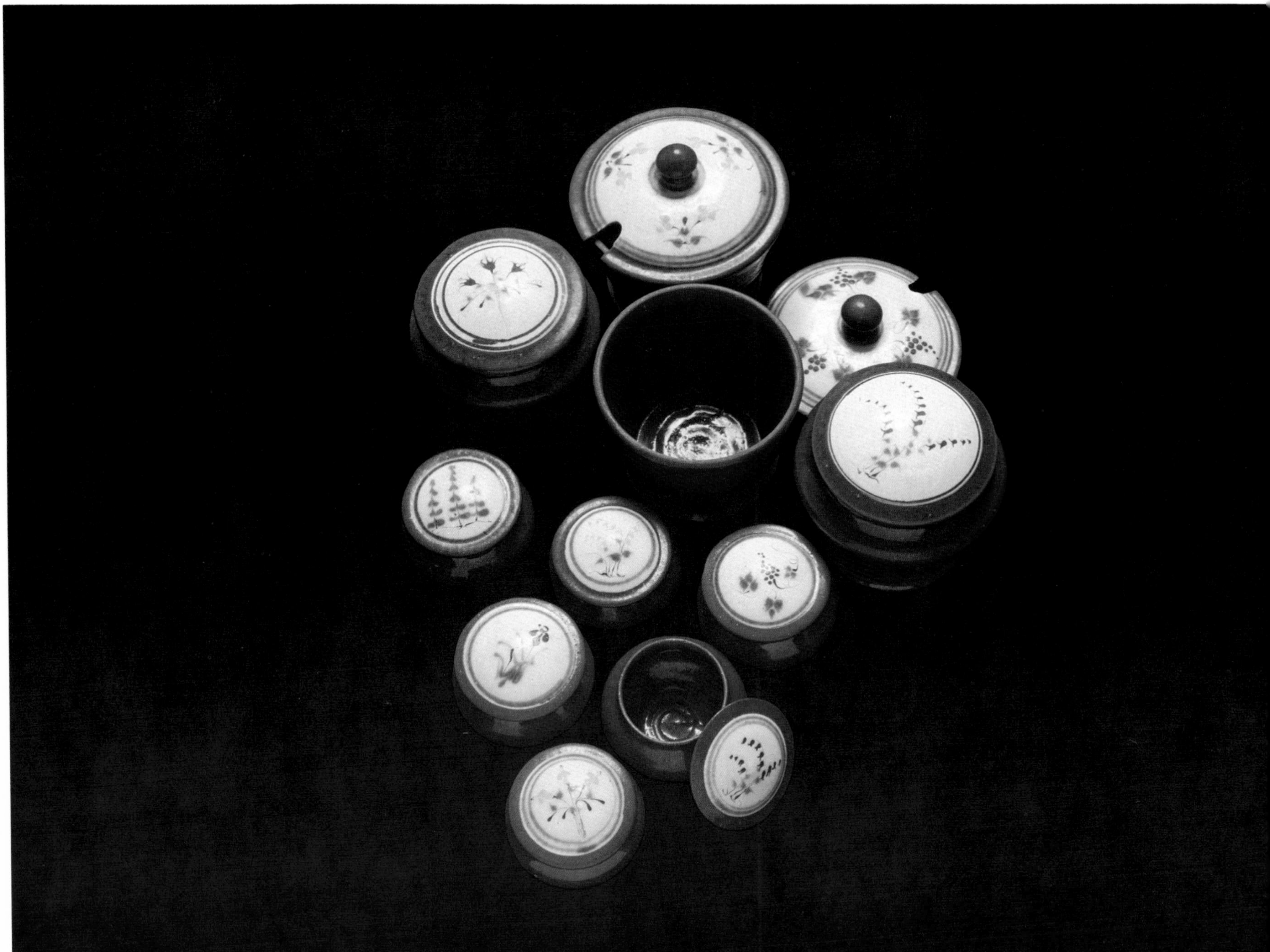

Monique Bourbonnais Ferron

Monique Bourbonnais Ferron

The mysterious technique of raku firing seems well suited to the spontaneous personality of Monique Ferron. She thrives on the split-second timing and the unpredictable impact of the elements. For the past ten years her energies have been devoted to exploring this ancient Japanese firing method, and the results have earned her a widespread reputation as a creative and responsive rakuist. She is noted particularly for her unique raku murals.

She began her career working a few hours a week with the well established Quebec potter Maurice Savoie, whose studio was just down the road from her home in Longueuil on the south shore of Montreal. At the time this was a fortunate arrangement for Monique who was busy keeping house and raising three daughters. For three years she trained with Savoie, doing handbuilt stoneware primarily, and then used this influence and knowledge as a stepping stone to develop her own style and begin her own studio production.

Her interest in raku evolved gradually, beginning as an experiment and becoming an all-consuming passion. In the early years she carried her brick raku kiln like a suitcase to a summer cottage in the Laurentians. It was then that she discovered a more transportable material made from kaolin, a refractory material that could withstand 2000°F temperatures and weighed paratically nothing. With the help of her husband Paul she built a kiln from this material (fiberfrax) bound together with chicken wire.

Today, she no longer totes her raku kiln since most of the week is spent at her farmhouse in the Eastern Townships south of Montreal. Her studio, kilns and home are here in the rolling hills of this fertile farming area. The house is old, and in a constant process of renovation, but large enough to accommodate her family and friends who join her here on the weekend. She spends the week preparing her pieces and then Paul assists her with the firings on the weekend.

An open shed which was originally the stable on this old Loyalist farm property is ideal for raku firing. In it are four propane-fueled raku kilns of different shapes and an assortment of post-firing covers that range from handbuilt galvanized tin to salvaged sap buckets for the smaller pieces. A barrel full of rainwater stands ready to douse the molten pots.

It is here in this tranquil setting that Monique performs the magic of the raku firing throughout every season of the year. She loves the winter when the snow melts and sizzles against the heat of the pot. Often in her enthusiasm for the moment she forgets the piece, only to discover it in the spring when the blanket of snow has melted away.

Monique Bourbonnais Ferron

Monique Bourbonnais Ferron

"The seasons here are so changeable. It's a wonderful place to work. In the summer I work in the barn. It's all open and airy with the wind blowing through the open windows and swallows swooping around my head. It does influence my work in funny ways. I started doing little window shapes on pieces. But it can also be desolate and lonely out here during the week. I call this place 'Wuthering Heights'. When it's windy the whole house moans, and on moonless nights it's pitch black here; there are no lights anywhere. All my colours have changed since I've been working here. I often use a combination of orangey-pink and black which is just the colour of the sky when the light is reflecting on black clouds. In the spring the orchards are beautiful – all pink and mauve against a red sky at sunset. I only realize later, when I look at my work, that these things are influencing me.

The first person I ever saw working with clay was Gaétan Beaudin in North Hatley. I became fascinated. Then I met Maurice Savoie, and being able to work with him was very important. I was very influenced by him; one is always influenced by the master. His way of working with clay was sympathetic to my point of view. That is, that clay pieces can be functional, but they can also be artistic or 'pièces uniques'.

It took a while to find my own style. I realized that I was very influenced by my teacher, so I started to work with stoneware slabs because at that time Maurice was working with coils. I tried working on the wheel, but I really wasn't attracted by it. I sort of fight with the wheel. It goes too fast for me and just doesn't work for me at all.

The very first time I tried raku it fascinated me and I suppose there was something in it that responded to my feelings. The spirit of raku is completely different. There is the whole connection with Zen philosophy, with nature, simplicity, profundity and quietness. It attracts me because it encompasses the very essence of pottery, the direct impact of the elements. Control in raku means that you have to learn to react to the chance the elements provide.

Raku started in Japan in the 16th century as part of the tea ceremony. The great tea master of that period wanted to have vessels for the tea ceremony which would not have the high toned ping of stoneware or porcelain. He wanted a muffled tone because everything had to be very subtle, quiet and aesthetic. He discovered a Korean potter who had taken his pots out of the kiln too early and then cooled them very rapidly with the result that these pieces, when scratched with a fingernail, had a coarse muffled sound. This was considered to be an indication of the pot's spirit. This potter then began

to make bowls for the tea ceremony. He was married to a Japanese woman and their son took over from his father and was given the title Raku I. That was centuries ago, but the tradition has carried on and now the great master Kichizaemon is Raku XIV.

I became more and more involved with raku and was reading everything I could find on Zen philosophy and aesthetics. I discovered my glazes in John Dickerson's book on raku and then I was fortunate enough to go to London and meet him. He is a professor at the Royal College of Art, and his thesis on raku is a very important work. He works in a very traditional way making tea bowls and ceremonial utensils.

In 1978 I went to Berkeley, California and took part in a Paul Soldner workshop. He was the originator of post-firing reduction, which is not part of the traditional Japanese raku method. He discovered it quite by accident one day when he took a piece out of the kiln and put it on the ground where it fell into some leaves. He found this created a different effect because there was some reduction taking place. He went on from there to develop post-firing techniques. Watching him work was very satisfying because it confirmed some of my own ideas on raku. It made me more sure of myself. He was working the way I do, although his style is completely different and very contemporary. But the technique is just the same. For post-firing reduction I use hay, leaves or pine needles – it doesn't really make much difference in the results.

What I like about raku is, first of all, that it is always different. There is always an element of surprise. Of course if you just put a white glaze on a black body and use the same reduction it will turn out black and white, but I always work in a crazy way trying out new things all the time. I only use three or four glazes, but I apply different layers, oxides or chlorides, and use different techniques of application which change the colour and texture effects. It is not in my nature to keep repeating the same thing. I sometimes worry about changing my style all the time. Maybe it is a fault. I seem to work for a while on many pieces in the same style and then I change. The changes are often caused by outside influences – like the colours of the landscape here – but sometimes they come from something that I see happening in a corner of a plate, for instance. I'll try it on another piece and then something new develops from that.

I am planning to build a stoneware kiln here and go back to making some slab-built, sort of sculptural things in stoneware. They won't be totally sculptural since I always tend to make things that have some use. They may still be functional in the sense that there

Monique Bourbonnais Ferron

might be a hole in the top to put weeds into. I don't think you can come to sculpture that easily. You can't say, "Today I am a potter; tomorrow I am a sculptor." Although I wouldn't call myself a potter either. I guess I am a ceramic artist. I think you can be a very great potter and a poor ceramic artist, or the other way around. It is the final product which determines what you really are. It bothers me that ceramics is still considered a secondary art in this country. But I think it is changing now. I have some of my pieces in the Montreal Museum of Fine Art, and some have been bought by collectors and galleries. When this sort of acceptance takes place, it means that things are changing.

When I go back to stoneware I will work in an entirely different way because of my experience with raku. With raku one is working with more freedom because you have to free your mind from pre-conceived design and just let yourself go. I had to train myself to become free. I did a lot of brushwork, first with ink on paper, and then I closed my eyes and painted so that it became second nature. When I first worked in stoneware I used to draw a form, then make the coils and build the form exactly like the drawing. Now I do stoneware forms that are much freer. I could never work in that constrained way again.

However, I think it was good for me to have this background of controlled work. I remember when I was about 12 years old and I went to a Catholic boarding school, we had drawing lessons. For days on end we did exercises – charcoal drawings of an orange, a bottle or any plaster form. I found it too dull. I wanted to do something else, I wanted to paint. But now I think it was not bad. It sort of educated one's hand.

Lately I have had shows twice a year. My work schedule is very constant. I feel divided sometimes between the city and this place, but now I am spending more time here and it gets easier. My husband always helps me with the firings and he likes to do odds and ends. He built this studio, including some of my tools. He made some brushes out of moosehair. He is a physician and has his practice in Longueuil, so he can't be here all the time, but he is always supportive and helpful.

There are so many things I want to do in ceramics, so many possibilities. I will keep doing raku, but sometimes I need a change. I am going to go back to stoneware. The raku experience has given me something that I want to transfer to stoneware. Stoneware is so beautiful – more solid, durable, indestructible by time or elements. At the same time, this permanence is somehow disquieting. Whatever I do with clay will be rewarding, however, because research and experiments can be adventures that open new paths. "

Maurice Savoie

Maurice Savoie

The Quebec poet and author Roch Carrier describes Maurice Savoie as a 'poète de la céramique'. Maurice creates ceramic masterpieces through his love of clay like a poet whose love of language creates written masterpieces. When he was only seven years old, he was given a tiny jar filled with clay. He treasured this gift and can still remember the delight of working with that clay as it responded to the touch of his small fingers. Years later, when he went into a pottery studio for the first time, it was the smell of the clay that attracted him. Again, it was the sensual aspect of this material that most impressed him and convinced him to become a ceramist. And today, after a lifetime of working with clay, he still is motivated by a sensitivity to this material.

Maurice was among the early vanguard of Quebec potters whose work and devotion to the craft set the stage for a whole generation of younger potters. There were very few resources for a struggling potter in the early fifties in Quebec and Maurice was fortunate in having scholarships to study in Faenza, Italy and to apprentice with master potter Francine Delppierre in Paris. These European experiences, the discovery of handbuilding in Paris, plus his interest in art history and archeology have given Maurice a cosmopolitan and experimental approach to his art.

Since 1959 he has worked in the basement studio of his home in Longueuil on the south shore of Montreal. His wife Suzanne was one of his first students years ago in Sherbrooke. She gave up ceramics, feeling that one in the family was enough, and now, after raising two sons, she manages the Centrale d'Artisanat in Montreal. The Savoie home is a showcase of Maurice's talent. In the living room a fireplace of floor to ceiling ceramic tiles creates a stunning focal point, while slab-built lamps and animal sculptures grace the tops of antique pine tables.

His studio reflects the order and serenity with which he approaches his craft. The tools are clean and everything is in its place. A contemplative man, he creates with a certain joy, usually with a smile on his face. The clay responds to this intimacy as it comes to life at his fingertips.

Maurice Savoie

A work of art is made because there is a love for the material. It is not possible to create something with a material one doesn't love or understand. A profound knowledge of the material is also necessary. One has to work a long time with clay before it finally gives up its secret. One can quickly become a clever potter, but it takes years to become a sensitive potter.

I have always approached ceramics in an experimental way. Even when I had my first studio in Sherbrooke I was making very sculptural, really very daring kinds of things. I guess I had been influenced by my teacher, Pierre Normandeau, at the École du Meuble where I studied ceramics. He was really a sculptor, not a potter. I have never been a real potter. I've tried and I think it is a most beautiful activity, but I just couldn't do it. I felt guilty for a long time about that, but I think it's my sense of curiosity that keeps pushing me further to try out new things instead of developing the discipline to keep repeating the same shape. One-of-a-kind pottery or ceramic sculpture seems better suited to my nature.

The early years were quite hard because there was no market; there were no craft shops in Quebec at that time. One man who was very supportive of me and my work was Jean-marie Gauvreau who was head of the Centrale d'Artisanat at the time. I brought some of my ceramics from Sherbrooke to Montreal to show him and he bought everything I had. It was my biggest sale up to that point and I was very proud. He was responsible for getting me the scholarship to study in Faenza. There were hardly any students or craftsmen travelling to Europe in those days, so this was quite exceptional.

It was while I was in Faenza that I really learned how to be a potter. I found out that I did not know how to throw properly and at this school there were children – 10 or 12 years old – who were throwing pots all day long following the model given to them by the master. I decided to start all over again and learn it. It was while I was there that I also developed a taste for faïence and majolica. These methods are seldom used over here because they are not in our tradition or in the British or Japanese tradition. But I like colourful ceramics and majolica really appealed to me.

When I came back from Europe I started teaching ceramics at the École du Meuble. It was tough because I was very young – almost as young as the students – and my training was more as an artist than as a craftsman. In those days you had to be either a potter or an artist and I was regarded as a maker of "céramiques de salon" because I was making one-of-a-kind pieces. I was criticized a lot and had to work hard at teaching as well as possible. It got to the point where there was no time for me to do my own creative work, and I cannot live without doing ceramics. I thought I would go crazy, so I decided to quit the job.

I started then with my own studio which was a big risk because I had a wife and a baby at the time, but I felt it was an important decision for my own stability. I was doing handbuilding and working long hours, night and day. I had mainly private clients and I was selling everything at ridiculous prices. At the same time I was teaching small groups of students in my studio.

About 10 months after I started I got my first commission for a mural from an architect. This was very important for me and I got many more contracts after this. I enjoyed making murals because my sculptor side was coming out, and it was also very economically rewarding. After a while I became known more as a muralist than a ceramist or a potter, purely through circumstance.

Over the years I have tried almost every level of teaching and the thing I find disturbing is that the emphasis is always on the technical aspects of ceramics. I feel that techniques are something that have to be learned, but not retained as the most important aspect. In schools there is too much insistence on techniques and unfortunately all it creates is very clever people with no sensitivity. This is very visible in the market. There are some spectacular ceramics which are very well done but they are dry; they have no feeling. The cultural aspect is never taught and I don't think you can separate art from a way of life or a culture because it all goes together. I am teaching now at the Visual Arts Centre once a week and I try to get the students to understand the sensitivity and the possibilities of their media. I am trying to make them *see* when they look at something. It seems to me that people keep looking at things without seeing. It is very hard to teach this. It would be much easier to teach straight techniques.

I think it would be wise for Canadian schools to hire more European teachers. We have to remember that ours is a new civilization and I feel very strongly about multiple influences. Young students tend to reject this notion and think they will invent everything themselves. Maybe I had an advantage with a North American education and then a European one as well. I think all this variety makes more of a whole.

The main questions I get asked by students are, "How can I create things? And why?" I don't think one can teach people the secret of how to express your feelings. I think everybody is born with a certain amount of talent which could be expressed in many ways. There are people who have more of this talent than others and these are the people we label artists. The two things you can't teach are motivation and sensitivity.

Maurice Savoie

Maurice Savoie

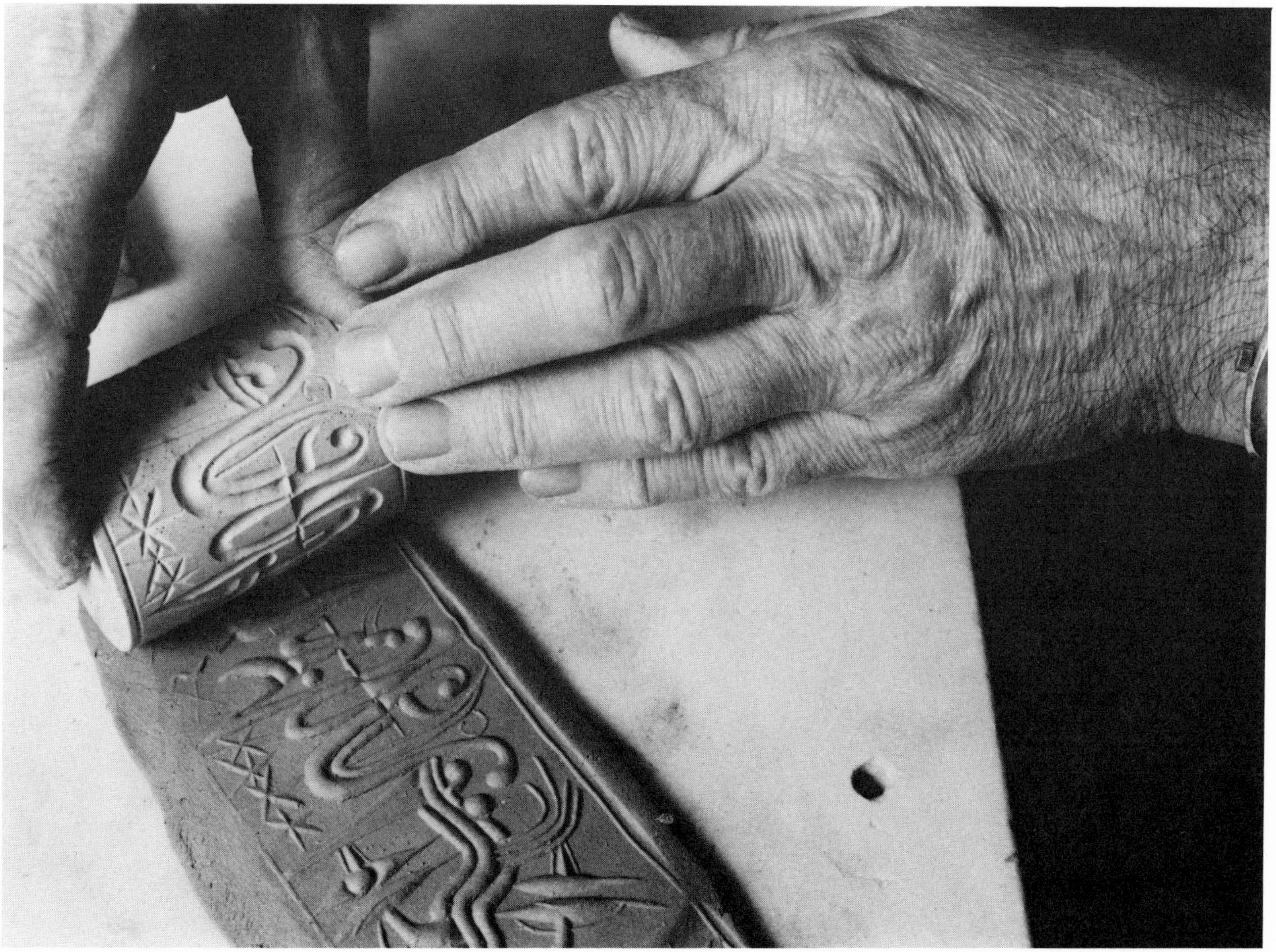

Maurice Savoie

Sometimes I feel it is more important for me to stay in my studio and achieve certain things in ceramics than to go out and teach. Maybe I am getting older and I am aware that time is getting shorter and I still want to do a lot of things. I am still searching for the form it should take. I feel I am more of a sculptor than a potter. I am just on the edge of that barrier. I am an artist, I am a craftsman – I don't know. I have been so influenced by my early years that I still consider function is important. When I am asked, "What is a piece for?" I still feel guilty saying it is a sculpture. Perhaps I should have the courage to get over this.

I try to use natural ingredients as much as I can. I use sand and smooth rocks to shape and give texture to clay forms. I take advantage of the machines and equipment that are available now, and I don't feel guilty about it. Take my slabroller, for instance. I made tiles and slabs by hand for many years for many, many murals. Therefore, I am ready now to have a slabroller. It is time saving and the time I save I use to express myself, which is more important now than making tiles by hand. My main preoccupation is to express an idea so I use the material or the tools that are best to make that expression.

I find that the influence of historical ceramic traditions keeps coming into my work. I am very impressed with Mesopotamian pottery and by the use of stamps in that culture. I have started to explore that technique. I use stamps to make stamps and I get a positive and a negative impression this way. When I am carving into the plaster I like to create a little story to keep myself amused. I try not to be too serious when I'm creating. Sometimes I catch myself 'playing the artist' and I have to stop myself. Picasso said we must create like children. Children do not create, but they play. They are more concerned with the act of creation than with the result.

When I do ceramics I feel I am touching something living. It moves, it teaches you something, it gives you something. It is very hard to explain with words because it is an unexplainable pleasure. It becomes a need, a part of you. It is like a great love and you have to be engaged with it all the time. This is the only way to achieve anything with it. You can't do ceramics as a part-time job.

Maurice Savoie

Clay imposes a great discipline. If you make the slightest mistake or if you omit something it will not necessarily revenge itself, but it *will* tell you. The relationship is very intimate. And it is so complex. You have to cope with fire, water, earth and air and it doesn't always give what you want. Sometimes when I get exasperated I think I would prefer to be a painter. Painting is a much more immediate art. But, on the other hand, when you open your kiln and the results are good (even if they're not the ones you expected) you have such an emotional feeling. And that's irreplaceable. "

Tim Worthington & Pam Birdsall

On the main street of Mahone Bay, Nova Scotia there's a forest green house bordered with cream trim and filled with the slip-trailed earthenware pots of Tim Worthington and his wife and partner Pam Birdsall. A handpainted sign, 'Birdsall-Worthington Pottery', hangs over the front door. Two large picture windows display their finely crafted wares. Across the street is the bay made famous by the three churches standing side by side at the water's edge. This sleepy Maritime community attracts tourists by the hundreds during the summer months, then empties like a burst dam after Labour Day. The four hundred year-round residents regard with pride the hard work and ingenuity of these two young potters, despite the fact they are not natives of Mahone Bay.

Tim was studying pharmacy in his native Ohio when he realized pharmacy was not for him. He came to the Nova Scotia College of Art and Design to do a Master of Fine Arts degree in ceramics. When he met Pam, she was an art student at the same college. Over the years, the decisions were made to marry, form a partnership, give up teaching positions, work together in earthenware, and find a place to live, work and sell their pottery. The latter proved to be the most difficult.

They had hoped to obtain grants to help finance the purchase and renovation of a pottery studio, but when this failed Pam's parents came to the rescue by forming a limited company and selling preferred shares to friends and acquaintances. Even some of Pam's and Tim's impoverished friends bought a few of the $10 shares to help them out. Apart from giving them the financing they needed, this commitment by others was a great boost for their morale. With so many people behind them they knew it was going to work. It *had* to work.

But it wasn't easy. In late 1976 they found the house in Mahone Bay. The location was perfect – right on the main street – but the building was in derelict condition. With grit, determination and a large dose of naive romanticism, they set to work. Living with no heat, no plumbing and no guarantees, they worked every weekend to convert the old abandoned house into what is now a charming combination of pottery shop, studio and home. In July of 1977 they opened their door for business.

Tim Worthington & Pam Birdsall

Pam: I'll never forget the night before we opened. We hadn't slept for three days. I was tending our first bisque firing and I fell asleep, allowing it to overfire. We opened it the next day and the upper third was all right, but the rest had all melted. I thought to myself, "Oh God, is this an omen?"

Tim: We can look back and laugh at these things now, but the first two years were really tough. We worked seven days a week and hardly ever left this building.

Pam: When we first opened here the response wasn't great. The pots were not wonderful and nobody knew we were here. At the time we weren't adding any colorant to the slip. It was still just yellow and brown. Everything in the shop was just yellow and brown.

Tim: It was fine when you took them out of the kiln separately. Or a piece on a wooden table looked nice. But when you had them all together, all you saw was a mass of brown. They all blended in and you couldn't see anything.

Pam: The craft shows were disasters. Our stuff looked terrible. It just needed a lot of presentation. We learned from that.

Tim: We found that people either really liked our pots because they were different or they wondered why we didn't have a blue or green to match their carpet!

Pam: The pots just didn't sell themselves. It took a lot of talking. Fortunately some people in this area related to our work because there are a lot of antique English slip-trailed milk bowls around here, so they had a reference point. We were very scattered at this time and I think our work reflected that. We were making pots all right but at the same time trying to install our bathroom and get our kitchen working. We really hadn't set up any concentrated exchange with our work.

Tim: It takes a while to get it all together. I remember one day the realization hit: "We are potters. This is our life and we better do it well!" It was then that we started to get away from all the yellow and brown. We added more coloured slips and began to feel much more comfortable with our craft. And the pots reflected that. They had much more feeling.

Pam: They became more personal, it seems. And we learned, too, that we had to listen to people in the shop in order to meet their needs. There's a tendency for art students to be arrogant and think that the public should be able to understand what you're doing. We had to get over that and if someone came to the shop and asked for a butter dish, we'd start making butter dishes. After all, we are production potters.

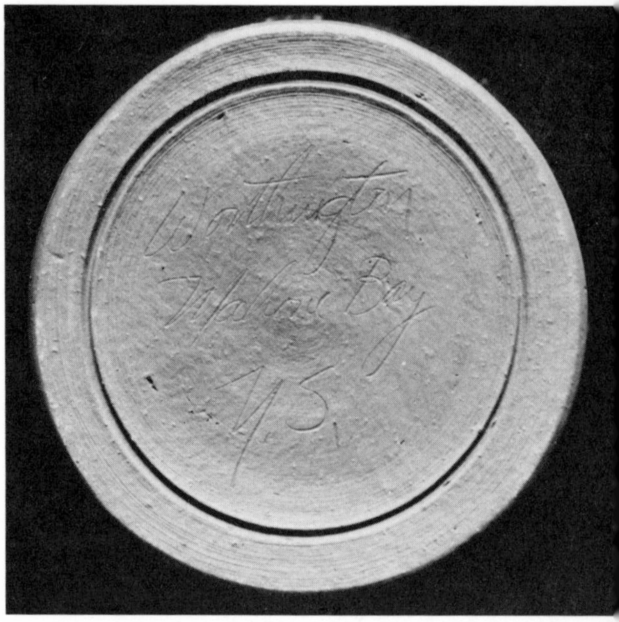

Tim: We learned a lot from using the pots ourselves. At college we never used what we made. Consequently, you never knew how deep to make a bowl in order not to eat cereal for two hours. These things we only learned when we replaced our K-Mart dishes with our own.

Pam: The decision to work in earthenware evolved slowly. I had started using it when I was teaching, then later working in Mom's basement. Then I saw Robin Hopper give a workshop and he did just a few tiles with slip decorating and honeycombing. This was the first time I'd seen it done and it impressed me so much that when I started using earthenware, sliptrailing was the first thing I did. I put a white ground down and used a feathering technique right away. It has certainly changed a lot since then.

Tim: At this time, I was working with Pam and going to graduate seminars at the college where most people were involved in fine arts. They were very up on contemporary arts and I was twisting myself inside out trying to make my work more 'intellectual'. It took a lot of rationalizing to finally feel all right about just making pots. At the same time I was reading a book called *The Unknown Craftsman*, all about folk art in Japan. It had a tremendous effect on me. The attitude of the people was not to think 'good or bad' or 'right or wrong'. They just made pots.

Pam: It's the unconscious approach. The refining of techniques which happens as you throw. Like when you put down your signature you don't think how to spell your name, it just flows. The whole thing is trying to tune into refining your craft and tools.

Tim: Anyway, all this blended together. It was going to be earthenware.

Pam: That also put things in context. By this time, I was a small-time production potter out of the basement, selling to a few shops. Tim had finally come to grips with being a production potter and not part of the 'New York contemporary conceptual scene'. The prospect of having a studio together was much closer.

Tim: So it all came about. Now that we've survived the first hard years we are able to relax a little more. Our work is selling well. Earthenware is well accepted down in this area. It is all local Nova Scotia clay so it's readily available. There seems to be a trend away from stoneware here.

Pam: People know that our clay is local clay and they like that. It is sort of 'home-grown'. Other studio potters in the area are doing earthenware too, but they don't do slip-trailing. Nobody does exactly what we do. And even if they did, it wouldn't be the same.

Tim: This is the interesting thing about pottery. Even if you tell someone else exactly

how to do what you're doing and give them the formula, theirs won't be the same as yours. You don't horde your trade secrets.

Pam: Secrecy is an attitude that can be dangerous. There is nothing new in clay. It has all been done before to a certain extent. It's personal variations that make pots exciting.

Tim: People often wonder how we can work and live together like this. It is hard sometimes and you have to get out. But in another way it is much easier when two people share the work. I'm not sure if I would do it by myself. Pottery is a labour-intensive thing. This way we can both work comfortably and have the volume of two potters. We don't have to throw twenty boards a day each.

Pam: There is a very delicate balance of two people working together. We happen to have an incredibly good working relationship in spite of seeing each other twenty-four hours a day. I guess it works because we like each other.

Tim: Now that things are going well we've thought about taking on somebody to help out in the studio mixing glazes or something. Not an apprentice, just an assistant.

Pam: One of the problems with doing greenware decoration is you have to be around a lot. The timing is crucial. For instance, mugs are dipped in the white slip and the first part to dry is the lip and the handle. If it dries too much, the slip doesn't adhere and just flakes off. You have to adjust to that. And it varies according to the heat and humidity. It has to be watched closely. It keeps you housebound sometimes. Days can go by and I realize that I have not been out, only up and down the stairs in this building. Tim goes out to the mailbox every day, but that's not a lot of outside activity.

Tim: I think we're just getting to the point where we can take time out without feeling guilty. I'm thinking of building a boat. It will be a small boat that we can row or sail and then we'll have access to all the little islands out in the bay. It seems a waste to live right across from the water and not have it as part of your life.

Pam: Tim has always been interested in boatbuilding and woodworking and building model airplanes. I think this is another factor in our being able to live and work together – our outside interests are different and we really do our own thing in pottery. We throw and decorate our own pieces. We share the same clay, coloured slips and clear glaze, but our work is still different.

SHEILA & STEPHEN
AUGUST 31, 1979

Tim Worthington & Pam Birdsall

Tim: The only thing we collaborate on are the large commemorative plates. Pam does the slip-trailed design in the centre and I do the sgraffito lettering around the rim. These plates are a very traditional English thing. They used to be ordered by the poorer people who couldn't afford a painter's portrait for a wedding. It's interesting to do them partly because of this tradition, but also because they provide a cultural documentation that will be around for a long time.

Pam: The other thing that's been really nice about these plates is that we've done a lot of them for local people here in Mahone Bay. They order them for weddings or Christmas. Some are ordering them now with drawings of their home with the family name and the date.

Tim: It's nice when the local people take an interest and want to buy your work. One day a man came in and wanted to have a bean crock made. A really big bean crock. He said that his wife makes a pot of beans every week and that's all they eat. I knew that he didn't have much money, so I suggested that he could probably get a bean pot for less money in the department store. But he didn't want that. He said that even if it cost him $25 he wanted me to make one for him.

Pam: Neither of us have ever lived in a small community like this before and it is really nice in a lot of ways. Everybody seems to think of us as their 'hometown potters'. We feel very rooted here. When Tim came to Halifax he had this romantic notion about living near the sea. It really fulfilled a lot of things for him. Often if you have a vision of a place it falls short, but this doesn't. Halifax was my home territory, but when the two of us came to Mahone Bay it was like a fresh start. We claimed it together. We are both new here and we share the same kind of feelings about it.

Kimberlie
Lucas Ross
March 8, 1979
George S.

Walter Ostrom

Walter Ostrom

For a potter the pursuit of his craft presents a myriad of paths to follow. In fifteen years Walter Ostrom has been down many of them. He has done stoneware and porcelain, raku and salt glazing, handbuilt sculptures and thrown pots, earthenware and majolica, all because he believes that it takes many, many years to become a potter and that one should experiment and experience as much as possible.

As a child growing up in New York State, Walter dreamed of becoming a scientist. He didn't discover clay until, as a chemistry student at the University of Buffalo, he spent hours between classes making pots in the student union building. When he went to Scotland to study chemistry and marine biology at the University of St. Andrews, he spent more time doing pottery at the nearby art college and ended up in Oland, Sweden on a ceramics scholarship. Back in the United States, he did graduate work with a Chinese potter, Henry Lin, at Ohio State University.

His interests in science and art have blended together for Walter into two obsessions: pottery and plants. His home on the barren seacoast of Nova Scotia is surrounded by rock gardens sprouting the fruits of his experiments with dwarf rhododendrons and alpine rock plants. His greenhouse and pottery studio are combined in a natural rock shed with huge slanted windows that let in the sun and look out on the ocean.

The grey clapboard house where he lives with his family has the weatherbeaten appearance of a fisherman's shack. Inside, the decor is austere, but splashes of colour from the decorative majolica pottery that is Walter's current interest create a feeling of warmth. The house began as one room where Walter lived as a bachelor, working at his wheel in a clothes closet. It then grew in stages with the addition of his wife Elaine, and then three children. Two cats, chickens, ducks, geese and a Newfoundland dog complete the ebullient Ostrom menagerie at Indian Harbour.

For the past five years every summer has been spent building something, often with the help of friends and family in the old tradition of barnbuilding. His studio-cum-greenhouse is made entirely from rocks collected on his property. It was an onerous task, but the result was a building that blends perfectly into the bleak windswept landscape of the Atlantic coast.

As head of the Ceramics Department at the Nova Scotia College of Art, Walter spends four days a week commuting to Halifax. It was the reputation of this school as a progressive institute that first brought him to Nova Scotia in 1969.

Walter Ostrom

"While I was doing my master's degree at Ohio State University, we had a visiting artist from the Nova Scotia School of Art come to lecture. I was impressed with the idea of the school, so I applied and got a job teaching art history part-time and ceramics part-time.

I had been offered a job at the university in Ohio, but there was no way I wanted to stay there. I was considered very strange in those days. I used to wear wooden shoes, round glasses and long hair, and they all wore bermuda shorts. I got beaten up a lot because I was anti-war. I remember I made a sculpture out of railroad iron and chains and the fraternity people attacked it and painted "communist pinko" all over it.

When I came to Nova Scotia, I moved right here to Indian Harbour. I liked this road. Peggy's Cove is just around the corner and it was the strangest environment I had ever seen in my life. It looked like a place on the moon. Elaine is from this area. She was the first student I ever dated. I taught one summer out in Saskatchewan and she needed a ride out there. I was very proper in those days. I wanted to be a conscientious teacher, but there we were out in the middle of nowhere and I thought nobody would ever know. So we dated and that was it. We ended up getting married.

When I first started teaching in Halifax, the conceptual art business was very strong and I was affected by this. I took all the wheels out of the department and instead of making pots we did all these projects. We had people hanging out of the window of the president's office on the sixth floor with ropes covered in clay. Then came the computer program. This project arose from my interest in glaze chemistry. We programmed a computer to print out all the theoretical glazes possible from cone 8 to 12 and ended up with about 2,000 glazes in two big volumes of printout pages. It became an exhibition piece and was shown in a gallery in Amsterdam where they pasted the gallery walls with all of these printout pages. The idea behind it was to show in some kind of physicality the actual formula of the glazes out of the theories. I guess it was a gesture to make the infinite finite.

Another project we did with the students was the Shubenacadie Project. This is the name of a place in Nova Scotia famous for its clay. We took 100 grams of this clay, along with its chemical analysis, and sent it to people like Hamada and Leach and other potters and artists. Many strange things happened. The responses were really interesting. People did everything from eating it to burying it and plotting it on a map. We recorded all these responses and published a book.

After a while I realized that the students didn't understand the significance of what they were doing with all of these conceptual projects. The other thing was that I was dying to make pots and I was subverting this desire by buying all sorts of antique pots. I bought some Sung Dynasty and Oribe ware in a gallery in Boston and it took me a year to pay for them. It was crazy. And then I had a talk with a painter friend of mine who pointed out to me that there is a difference between ceramics and conceptual art. In ceramics we have an allegiance to a material and in conceptual art there is no allegiance to any material at all.

So all of this came together and I decided I was going to make pots. But then I had to rationalize to myself how to get back into pots again. I was so naive then. Or self-important! I decided that in order for students to understand the abstract way of dealing with a material they had to understand what a good pot is and what pottery, clay and kilns are all about. So I started to make pots – stoneware and raku at first. I was so happy to get back to the nuts and bolts of pottery. I think the students were relieved too.

Around this time I had my first one-man show in Toronto at the Potter's Guild. It was a combination of raku and salt-glazed stoneware. I was so excited. I remember the panic of setting up that show knowing that the people at the Guild assumed I was a very sophisticated person. I didn't even know what to charge or where to put things. My raku pieces were all pastel colours, pale yellows and pinks and blues. I hated the popular raku glazes, so I thought I'd do the opposite and be more subtle. Of course the response was, " Raku is earth and fire. Where are the copper reds and lustres?" I didn't sell much at the show. I really fell on my face.

I started working in earthenware after doing a workshop in the Annapolis Valley with some wonderful people. At the time I was into the mystique of high firing and they kept telling me that they had this low firing red clay and insisted that I do something with it. The first thing I thought of making was flower pots, so I made some right there, and then I brought some of the clay home with me. It was fantastic clay and it came right out of someone's backyard.

The clay I'm using now comes from a brick factory 40 miles from here. I just go and get it as it comes right out of the ground. I add some barium carbonate to it because it scums so badly. Right now I'm experimenting with adding a local red stoneware clay to make it better for ovenware.

Anyway, after being at this workshop I came home and began making unglazed flower pots for myself and they started selling well. That year I was on a sabbatical and

Walter Ostrom

Walter Ostrom

we had little money, so I potted every day making flower pots from 9 to 5. One of the problems I encountered with the unglazed earthenware flower pots was that the city water is so full of soluble salts that it goes right through the pot and leaves a white scum. I really didn't want to glaze them because I loved the look of the raw fired clay, so I came up with the idea of using terra sigillata as a compromise. It gives a very nice surface and is like a salt glaze in that it picks up every line.

During that same year I had a huge exhibition in Halifax with all these terra sigillata flower pots and half of them, at least, had plants and flowers in them. I had over 1000 bulbs planted. The whole effect was really beautiful, but a lot of work. I had forced azaleas and rhododendrons to bloom early with the help of the head of the agriculture department. It was quite an event. The show sold out on opening night.

Two days after the Halifax show I left with a group of people for China. I was the Maritime artist representative. I planned to go to Japan after China and spend two months there by myself. I had warned my wife that I would probably call her and say, "Rent the house, We're going to live in Japan for a while." You see Japan had been my dream country for years. I had studied oriental art history and I always thought that going there and seeing all those pots would be just wonderful.

So I went to Japan. I had one great day with Shoji Hamada and from then on it was downhill. The pots were garbage, just el garbogolo! It just wiped me out! I only stayed one month and came home so discouraged I thought I would never make a pot again.

On the first trip to China I didn't see any pottery, but then I went back again with a group of potters and found some very positive things there. The society there could not exist without pottery. If all the potteries in China stopped today the country would collapse because everything, all their containers, are made of clay.

So these trips to the East really affected me. I realized that if you live in a third world country you have to come to grips with reality. I had all these mystiques about living in the country, making pots, subverting the aesthetics of the world with the cornflake bowl, that sort of thing. I learned in the Orient that what I related to was totally different from what they related to.

I started at rock bottom. I made flower pots for my garden, terrines and bowls for the kitchen, chicken feeders – all things for the house. Because I was using earthenware and decorating with engobe, I started to research the technology of this. I just started doing majolica recently. I really love folk pottery and would like to go to Italy, take a couple of test tiles of my own, and compare all kinds of majolica whites. If I just work here with my materials and in my studio, I am only going to get certain results. And that's frustrating.

Right now I am trying to establish limits for myself, and one of them is utility. I think utility can be a dynamic way of generating forms. It can go beyond whether a lid fits. I like to consider what the food is going to look like when I put it into a pot. Like with my candy jars; I decorate them with candy shapes and colours. Right now I'm working on jugs to hold plastic milk bags. These are an example of the new demands being put on a potter because of how our culture has changed.

One thing that has changed in ceramics since I first began is the hierarchy of the media. Ten years ago, there were pressures to do something in a certain way. When I was a student, it was stoneware in the anglo-oriental tradition. Then, five years ago, there was all kinds of pressure to do arty earthenware – white talc bodies with California narrative. If you were 'with it', you had to do this or that. I don't think it makes any difference anymore. There has been a real renaissance of the container in the last few years. And now just because you do earthenware it doesn't mean you are any less serious than someone who does porcelain.

I have been through many changes of style and I know it can be a liability. The galleries aren't happy when your work keeps changing because they want to know what they are getting. But I never forget what my old Chinese teacher Henry Lin said when I went to him on a bad day and asked if he thought I could ever be a good potter. He said, "Walter, give yourself forty years. If you make pots for forty years and you have something to contribute to pottery, it will show. If you have nothing to contribute to pottery, you will be an expert in your field." So I give myself forty years. I figure when I'm in my fifties I will be getting to my mature period. In the meantime, what I want to do is investigate. "

Walter Ostrom

Glossary

AGATEWARE
clay body resembling agate-stone in appearance

AIR-BRUSH DECORATION
spraying glaze by means of compressed air

ASH GLAZE
a glaze containing large proportions of tree or plant ashes, usually fired at high temperatures

BARIUM CARBONATE
a chemical substance added in small quantities to earthenware clay bodies to prevent discoloration

BISQUE FIRE
first firing of greenware without glaze

BISQUE WARE
unglazed, once-fired ceramic ware

BIZEN WARE
originally an unglazed, red-bodied stoneware produced in Japan's historical 'six old kilns' district

CERAMIC STAINS
stable colorants used as overglaze and underglaze decorations and clay body colorants

COIL BUILDING
hand building ceramic shapes using ropelike rolls of clay

CONE
a term generally used to indicate a specific temperature marking the end of firing

CRAZING
excessive crackling of glaze

EARTHENWARE
porous pottery that matures at a low firing temperature

ELECTRIC KILN
a kiln generally fired to oxidation and fueled by electricity

ENGOBE
white or coloured clay slip used to decorate green or bisque ware

EXTRUDER
a hand or electrically powered machine for forcing clay through an opening into a desired shape

FAÏENCE
earthenware covered with tin enamelled glaze. Also, a term for earthenware originally produced in Faenza (Italy) during the Renaissance, imitating Spanish majolica ware

FEATHERING
a method of decorating by lightly scraping through slips on a wet pot

FETTLING
trimming or smoothing rough edges of leather hard pieces before firing

GAS KILN
a reduction kiln fueled by gas

GREENWARE
unfired, bone dry ceramic pieces

GLAZE
finely ground mineral compounds suspended in liquid and applied to bisque ware by pouring, brushing or spraying. When fired the ingredients melt together forming a vitreous surface

HAND BUILDING
creating ceramic shapes by hand forming as opposed to throwing on a wheel

HONEY COMBING
decorating by scoring the surface of ceramic pieces with fingers or a toothed instrument

KICK WHEEL
a foot-operated potter's wheel

KILN
a furnace of refractory material designed for firing ceramic objects and enamels, usually fueled by wood, gas or electricity

LEATHER HARD
partly damp ceramic ware still soft enough for carving or burnishing the surface

LUSTRE
low-fired metallic iridescent glaze

MAJOLICA
earthenware covered with a high gloss tin lead glaze; originally from Spain

MOLD
a form with which clay can be shaped; usually made from plaster of paris

NERIAGE
a clay body made in layers of contrasting colours; a technique originally developed in Japan

OVERGLAZE
decoration applied over a glazed ware

OXIDATION FIRE
a firing technique using a full supply of oxygen, generally in an electric kiln

Glossary

OXIDES
metal oxides of various origin used as colorants in clay bodies and glazes

PORCELAIN CLAY
a hard, non-absorbent, translucent clay body fired at high temperature

RAKU
an ancient Oriental ceramic technique using a groggy open clay body. The glazed bisqued raku ware is placed in a hot kiln. The glaze matures usually within 30 minutes, and the pieces are removed

RAKU KILN
a kiln especially built for firing raku ware. The chamber must be readily accessible and easily opened or closed with the kiln at full temperature

REDUCTION FIRED
a firing process using insufficient oxygen. The carbon monoxide thus formed from the heated clay and glaze produces colour changes in the glazed ware

REFRACTORY MATERIAL
a heat-resisting material

SALT GLAZING
a firing process involving throwing salt into a hot kiln to produce a particular glaze effect

SGRAFFITO
decorating leather hard slip covered pots by scratching through the slip to expose the contrasting body colour underneath

SHARD (SHERD)
a broken fragment of pottery

SLAB CONSTRUCTION
a method of building ceramic shapes with rolled or pressed sections of clay

SLAB ROLLER
a manually operated or motorized rolling machine which presses out even clay slabs of a desired thickness

SLIP
liquid clay in suspension

SLIP CAST
a ceramic process using plaster molds filled with liquid clay

SLIP DECORATION
decoration using techniques such as brushing, dipping, sgraffito, trailing, feathering and marbling on greenware

SLIP TRAILING
decorating a surface with a squeeze bottle or rubber syringe containing clay slip

STAMP DECORATING
impressing a design or pattern into clay with carved plaster stamps or other objects

STIPPLE
to engrave or roughen a smooth surface

STONEWARE
hard, nearly non-porous, high-fired (above cone 8) ceramic ware

TERRA SIGILLATA
reddish-brown, slightly glossy slip glaze, widely used in ancient times especially on Roman pottery

THROWING
forming ceramic shapes on a potter's wheel

UNSAGGERED
in a manner providing direct contact with the flame; usually used in wood firing

VITRIFICATION
a progressive fusion or glassification of clay during firing

WARPAGE
distortion of a clay shape caused by uneven shaping, drying or firing

WEDGING
kneading or pounding a clay body to remove air pockets, thereby developing a uniform texture

WHEEL
a rotating wheel used for throwing or hand forming ceramic objects. Manually powered historically, wheels are now mostly electrically operated

WHITEWARE
ceramic pieces made of a white or light cream coloured clay body

WOOD FIRING
a firing process using wood as a fuel

Colour Plates

cover A multiple-glazed porcelain vase slab-built and thrown by Robin Hopper.

33 Walter Ostrom's thrown earthenware jug is 13 cm high and has a majolica white glaze. It is seen against the sunset at Indian Harbour, Nova Scotia.

34 The flute-edged porcelain plate made by Keith Campbell of Corbeil, Ontario is about 35 cm in diameter and has an airbrushed design.

35 Ann Mortimer's raku plate, called 'Smoked Bird', is 35 cm in diameter.

36 The tallest of the porcelain storage jars wood-fired to cone 11 reduction by Ruth Gowdy McKinley is 19 cm high. Both show signs of ash flashing.

37 A collection of Roger Kerslake's salt-fired pieces. All are thrown and altered with handbuilt additions or extruded handles. They range from 33 to 46 cm in height.

38 Robin Hopper's porcelain slab bottle is 43 cm high. Multiple glaze applications have been used to evoke the feeling of the landscape.

39 One of Annemarie Schmid Esler's handbuilt pieces from her 'Crows in Crates' series. Completely handbuilt from white earthenware clay, the life-size crows are slip-cast.

40 Jack Sures' porcelain covered jar is 25 cm high and was thrown and handbuilt.

81 The studio of Wayne Ngan on Hornby Island, British Columbia.

82 Walter Ostrom in his studio at Indian Harbour. A collection of his pots includes terra sigillata flower pots, candy jars with engobe decoration and handbuilt earthenware serving dishes.

83 The range of John Chalke's work, including his multi-fired wall plates, is seen in the showroom of his Calgary, Alberta home.

84 Lorraine Herman at work on one of her handbuilt porcelain boxes in her studio in Kleinburg, Ontario.

85 Pam Birdsall and Tim Worthington in front of their home and pottery shop in Mahone Bay, Nova Scotia.

86 Gaétan Beaudin at the Sial factory in Laval, Quebec, with some of the ceramic line which he created and designed for industrial production.

87 Monique Bourbonnais Ferron at her farmhouse in the Eastern Townships of Quebec. In the foreground are some of her raku-fired pieces.

88 Byron Johnstad at work in his studio in Lantzville, British Columbia.

121 A selection of Roger Kerslake's pots in both stoneware and porcelaine. His studio, a converted barn in Jarratt, Ontario, is seen in the background.

122 Two of Jack Herman's thrown storage jars and a lidded casserole. All are reduction-fired stoneware with brushed or poured glaze application.

123 Maurice Savoie's zoomorphic-shaped vase with ash glaze is 38 cm high and was handbuilt with stoneware clay.

124 A variety of thrown stoneware colanders with tripod feet, wood-fired by Ruth Gowdy McKinley. Diameters range from 15 to 25 cm. All are glazed inside and ash-flashed outside.

125 Jack Sures' unglazed stoneware teapot is handbuilt and 30 cm high.

126 A collection of Pam Birdsall's covered jars made from Nova Scotian clay and decorated by slip trailing. The jars range from 5 to 12 cm in height.

127 Three of Lorraine Herman's handbuilt porcelain boxes. Whimsical figures adorn the lids of these containers which are about 13 cm high.

128 A collection of the raku work of Monique Bourbonnais Ferron. The handbuilt slab vase is 33 cm high; the large wall plate is 33 cm square.

Designed by Frank Newfeld

Text composed in Zapf Book,
Helvetica and Bank Script

Colour separations by
Herzig Somerville Limited

Printed and bound by
The Bryant Press Limited